Living *in the* Excellence *of* Jesus!

Cheryl Price, Ph.D.

UMI (Urban Ministries, Inc.)
Chicago, Illinois

Publisher
UMI (Urban Ministries, Inc.)
P.O. Box 436987
Chicago, Illinois 60643-6987
1-800-860-8642
www.urbanministries.com

First Edition
First Printing

Library of Congress Cataloging-in-Publication Data

Living in the Excellence of Jesus! / Cheryl Price, Ph.D.
Includes bibliographical references.
ISBN-13: 978-1-934056-64-6
ISBN-10: 1-934056-64-2
1. Christian living   2. African American

Library of Congress Control Number: 2007925595

Printed in the United States of America.

DEDICATION

This book is dedicated to Alexander and Sierra, my loving children, who were patient beyond their years in giving me research and writing time. And to the rest of my family, who have been there for me through the sunshine and rain in my life, I thank our gracious God for all of you!

TABLE OF CONTENTS

ACKNOWLEDGMENTS

I must pause and give great thanks to the excellence of Jesus in my life, and for using me to minister to His people.

In addition, I would like to thank C. Jeffrey Wright, president and CEO of UMI, for asking me to write this book and having faith in me. Many thanks to Dr. Banks, founder and visionary of UMI, for his support and prayers during this endeavor.

Completing the books (this, the workbook, and the leader's guide) would not have been possible without the great assistance of Mrs. Evangeline Carey. Her dedication and diligence in serving as the editor were very valuable.

Others who assisted and made this project a reality were Miss Megan Bell, the competent and tenacious copy editor here at UMI; Mrs. Kim Brooks, who gave her time and energy to help as needed; and the entire UMI staff, who gave their support and prayers during very critical times of thinking and writing these books. Concurrently, I would like to thank Rev. Darryl Sims for his title suggestion and Rev. William Martin and Minister Marlin Jamison for their insights after reading the chapters.

Thank you to my friends, who always have a listening ear and sent prayers to our loving Jesus to help me make it through. Also special thanks to those who gave me spoken and unspoken words of encouragement in my time of instruction during the Fall 2006 "Ministers as Teachers" course at Howard University School of Divinity.

PREFACE

"O LORD our Lord,
how excellent is thy name
in all the earth!
who hast set thy glory above the heavens"
(Psalm 8:1, KJV).

"Praise ye the LORD.
Praise, O ye servants of the LORD,
praise the name of the LORD.
Blessed be the name of the LORD
from this time forth and for evermore.
From the rising of the sun
unto the going down of the same
the LORD'S name is to be praised"
(Psalm 113:1–3, KJV).

As you encounter *Living in the Excellence of Jesus!* it should help you to praise our God because indeed His name is excellent in all the earth!

INTRODUCTION

Living in the Excellence of Jesus! demands that we, as His disciples, pattern our lives after our Lord and Savior, and strive to be all that He is calling for us to be. In His Holy Word, as we follow His birth, ministry, death, and Resurrection, we find that Jesus came into this world for one purpose only, and that was to be the "Sacrificial Lamb," who would pay our sin penalty by dying on the Cross. He had a standard that He never strayed from, and that was excellence. He did not do anything half-measure, but stuck to His agenda, or purpose, to build His kingdom that will consist of every blood-washed believer reigning with Him in the New Jerusalem or on the New Earth.

From the true-to-life (Up Front and Personal) accounts, the biblical accounts (A Word from the Lord), and Something to Think About. . ., I pray that you will see this excellence of Jesus and strive to be a doer of His Word. In order to carry out the Great Commission—"Go and make disciples of all the nations, baptizing them in the name of the Father and the Son and the Holy Spirit. Teach these new disciples to obey all the commands I have given you" (Matthew 28:19–20, NLT)—we need to be salt and light (excellent examples) to a lost and dying world. This way, they will know how to talk as we show them the Jesus in us. We should show them changed lives—lives impacted by God's Holy Spirit living in us. It is His Holy Spirit that will help us graduate to great!

TRUSTING GOD IN THE UNEXPECTED

BASED ON LUKE 1:26–45

KEY VERSE: *"Gabriel appeared to [Mary] and said, 'Greetings, favored woman! The Lord is with you'"* (Luke 1:28, NLT).

UP FRONT AND PERSONAL

We cannot always trust what we read, hear, or see. In fact, some things in life are not always what they appear to be. In addition, some things may have a different meaning than what we initially thought. When we reflect on those quick judgments we may have made about someone or those times when we were wrongly judged and had to live with the consequences, we realize at a deeper level that we should think before we speak, and "we shouldn't judge a book by its cover." Because this is true in a variety of ways in our lives, we may discover that, intentionally or unintentionally, we have been misled or given the wrong information. This information may even become what we think is real, or truth.

Truth or understanding is sometimes covered up with clever words or can be lost in time. These two factors can conceal the real meaning. The famous Mother Goose nursery rhymes, which originated in England, are examples of how the original meanings become obscure. Popular nursery rhymes are catchy tunes that we teach to children; but do we really know what we are singing? Chris Roberts, in the book *Heavy Words Lightly Thrown: The Reason Behind the Rhyme*, reminds us that the real meanings behind particular nursery rhymes, at first reading, can be ambiguous (2005, xv). Remember the nursery rhyme "Little Jack Horner" (2005, 1)?

> Little Jack Horner
> Sat in a corner
> Eating his Christmas pie,
> He stuck in his thumb
> And pulled out a plum,
> And said, "What a good boy am I!"

Roberts states that Jack is thought to be a man named Thomas Horner, who is from Glastonbury, Britain (2005, 1). As you know, they did not have the mail carrier services that we do today. Instead, in this particular tale, the important documents were concealed in a pie. Jack's job was to take the pie, with the title deed concealed under the crust, to the king. There were in fact 12 deeds and it is alleged that Jack actually stole one of them, which is represented by "a plum" in the story. Thomas (Jack) delivered it to the king to persuade him to purchase property from the church—from one of the clergy, Abbott Richard Whittington. Mr. Horner's family denies that Thomas Horner ever stole the title deed, but he purchased the home (a mansion) that they live in today (2005, 2).

Another popular nursery rhyme is "Mary, Mary, Quite Contrary" (2005, 33).

> Mary, Mary, quite contrary,
> How does your garden grow?
> With silver bells and cockleshells,
> And pretty maids all in a row.

It is agreed that this nursery rhyme is about someone named Mary—which Mary and the actions of Mary are in question, though. One belief is that "the bells" and the "cockleshells" are connected to Our Lady's convent, which has the Sanctus bells. The cockleshells represented the badges worn by the pilgrims. These were not the pilgrims we recognize in the U.S. today, who were a part of the "English colony." Instead, they were pilgrims who lived in England (Plimoth Plantation, Inc. 2003, paragraph 2). Remember that many of the nursery rhymes and the Mother Goose Tales originated in England.

The "pretty maids" would be "the nuns in the service of Mary" (Roberts 2005, 33). Mary could also represent Mary, Queen of Scotland, who was not kind toward Protestants, and in fact persecuted them. The silver bells and the cockleshells are references to the instruments of torture, like thumbscrews, she used against her adversaries (2005, 35). The pretty maids could refer to the women who were left as widows when their husbands were killed by the queen's assassins (2005, 35).

After learning this information about Jack and Mary, maybe the next time you read or hear a nursery rhyme, you will ask what it really means and do your own research.

It can be hard to trust what we read and what we hear, at times. Like the printed word, popular or common phrases that began to hurt or harm someone now have a fresh and inoffensive connotation. Maybe you are more familiar with the phrases or words that were (are) very racist and degrading to African Americans. The term *cowboy* was used for "an African slave who tended the cows on a plantation in the southern territories or states. . . .'cowboy' was later used to refer to White cattlemen of the West" (Major 1994, 117). In the same light, folklore also tells us that many Whites in America referred the "Brazil" nut, which has a dark and rough textured outer covering, to the heels of Black people.

Additionally, according to folklore, the popular raising of one finger— while walking out of the sanctuary during a sermon or someone speaking— has its origin in U.S. slavery days. The raised finger was the sign that slaves had to use during worship services to signal to the slave's master that the slave was leaving during the worship service. Although people can see that we are leaving our seats and tipping out, today many African Americans churchgoers continue to practice this tradition as though it is a common courtesy and ritual. This polite tradition is usually practiced by adults, but children are seen emulating this slave tradition as well.

In this same light, in church, our understanding of God's Word is sometimes more defined by traditions than the Bible. Today, we are often guilty of misinterpreting and misunderstanding Scripture; thus, we reinterpret or recreate the Bible stories. The original meaning becomes intertwined or covered up with new traditions that begin to have as much credibility, or weight, as the real story or meaning. For example, the joyous Christmas play in many of our churches is usually told with the shepherds, the wise men, and possibly a drummer boy marveling at the birth of the newborn Baby Jesus. As the well-wishers marvel at Jesus' birth, Mary and Joseph— the parents—and some barnyard animals are quietly witnessing this miraculous birth. What a miracle it would be if we actually shared with those watching and participating in the play that the gospels of Matthew and Luke have been combined, and that the shepherds and the wise men were not there to witness the birth of Jesus. In fact, the wise men, exact number unknown, did not come until Jesus was at home and older than a newborn. Read Matthew 2:9–12 and Luke 1:15–18 and compare the two gospels for yourself. The drummer boy is not listed in any of the gospels, so we have added a new character on our own.

In this light, it is not uncommon for many Christians to use their "sanctified" imaginations to create a new story and a new meaning of Scripture, which is the all-knowing God's inerrant Word. However, as we strive for excellence, we want to know God's Word and get the God-intended meaning of Scripture. We want to know what God, the Creator of the universe and all that exists, actually says and not what we want Him to say.

A WORD FROM THE LORD
SCRIPTURE: Luke 1:26–45
PLACE: Judea
CHARACTERS: Mary, Joseph, Elizabeth, Zechariah

Luke 1:26, NLT In the sixth month of Elizabeth's pregnancy, God sent the angel Gabriel to Nazareth, a village in Galilee, **27** to a virgin named Mary. She was engaged to be married to a man named Joseph, a descendant of King David. **28** Gabriel appeared to her and said, "Greetings, favored woman! The Lord is with you!" **29** Confused and disturbed, Mary tried to think what the angel could mean. **30** "Don't be afraid, Mary," the angel told her, "for you have found favor with God! **31** You will conceive and give birth to a son, and you will name him Jesus. **32** He will be very great and will be called the Son of the Most High. The Lord God will give him the throne of his ancestor David. **33** And he will reign over Israel forever; his Kingdom will never end!" **34** Mary asked the angel, "But how can this happen? I am a virgin." **35** The angel replied, "The Holy Spirit will come upon you, and the power of the Most High will overshadow you. So the baby to be born will be holy, and he will be called the Son of God. **36** What's more, your relative Elizabeth has become pregnant in her old age! People used to say she was barren, but she's now in her sixth month. **37** For nothing is impossible with God." **38** Mary responded, "I am the Lord's servant. May everything you have said about me come true." And then the angel left her. **39** A few days later Mary hurried to the hill country of Judea, to the town **40** where Zechariah lived. She entered the house and greeted Elizabeth. **41** At the sound of Mary's greeting, Elizabeth's child leaped within her, and Elizabeth was filled with the Holy Spirit. **42** Elizabeth gave a glad cry and exclaimed to Mary, "God has blessed you above all women, and your child is blessed. **43** Why am I so honored, that the mother of my Lord should visit me? **44** When I heard your greeting, the baby in my womb jumped for joy. **45** You are blessed because you believed that the Lord would do what he said."

BACKGROUND

NAME: Mary, found in the New Testament as Maria or Mariam
FAMILY ORIGIN: King David
AGE: Under 18 years of age when pregnant and later married to Joseph
MARITAL STATUS: Later married to Joseph
OCCUPATION: Homemaker
CHILDREN: Jesus, James, Joseph, Judas, Simon, and daughters
RESIDENCE: Nazareth, Bethlehem

NAME: Joseph, which means "may he add"*
FAMILY ORIGIN: King David
AGE: Unknown
MARITAL STATUS: Married to Mary, the mother of Jesus
OCCUPATION: Carpenter
CHILDREN: Jesus (legally—not biologically), James, Joseph, Judas, Simon, and daughters
RESIDENCE: Egypt, Nazareth, Bethlehem
*Joseph was a man of compassion, a skilled worker, and a provider (Life Application Study Bible 1996, 1399).

NAME: Elizabeth, which means "My God has sworn"
FAMILY ORIGIN: the priestly line of Aaron
AGE: Unknown but elderly
MARITAL STATUS: Married to Zechariah
OCCUPATION: Homemaker
CHILDREN: John the Baptist
RESIDENCE: Judea

NAME: Zechariah, which means "Yahweh remembers" or "whom Yahweh remembers"
FAMILY ORIGIN: the priestly family—the order of Abijah
AGE: Unknown but elderly
MARITAL STATUS: Married to Elizabeth
OCCUPATION: Jewish Priest
CHILDREN: John the Baptist
RESIDENCE: Judea

The gospel writer Luke begins this section of his writing with a proclamation from Gabriel, who had been sent by God to share a very important and unique birth announcement. It was to be taken to a young woman named Mary, who lived in Nazareth, a village in Galilee. Gabriel's visit to Mary denoted that a major event was about to occur. Gabriel is one of only two angels that are named in the Bible. Gabriel's name means "God is my hero" or "mighty man of God" (Barker, et. al. 1995, 34). He is the angel named in Luke 1:19; Daniel 9:21. The other angel that is identified by name is "Michael," whose name means "the great prince who protects" and is found in Daniel 10:13, 21; Jude 9; and Revelation 12:7 (1995, 1306).

Mary's unusual story (or not), within the Judeo-Christian experience, invites us to hear the words of the angel Gabriel to Mary about a special blessing that God gave to her. Gabriel's surprise visit and words to Mary that she was "favored or blessed" among women and that "The Lord is with you" at first frightened her (Luke 1:28–29, NLT). Gabriel told Mary not to be afraid, that she had been chosen by God to be the mother of the promised Messiah, and that she was to name Him "Jesus."

It is important to note that Mary naming her baby *Jesus* was not insignificant. The name Jesus is the Greek form of the Hebrew name "Joshua." At the time, this was a common name and means "the Lord saves" (Life Application Study Bible 1996, 1932). As already experienced within an earthly context, when Joshua led the people into the Promised Land, Jesus' name represented Jesus leading "His people into eternal life." Scholars explained that Jesus' name was quite notable during this time because people took seriously the meaning of a name and "saw them as a source of power" (1996, 1932). As written throughout the New Testament and evidenced throughout time, the name of Jesus has power. Through His name, miracles of healing, deliverance, lives restored, forgiveness, and mercy were shown. Even sin had to bow to the power of His forgiveness (1996, 1932).

Jesus' conception and birth into the world brought about the fulfillment of God's promise to David for an everlasting kingdom (2 Samuel 7:16). As proclaimed by Gabriel, Jesus, the "Son of the most High," is "the divine son of God and the Messiah born in time" (Life Application Study Bible 1996, 1534). In time and for all eternity, what a miracle and a blessing for Mary to be selected by Almighty God for such a wonderful miracle! Although Mary heard about this marvelous miracle that would change her life and the world forever, she was surprised and perplexed as to how this could happen. She was startled and confused at what had been told to her because she asked and declared to Gabriel, "But how can this happen? I am a virgin" (Luke 1:34, NLT).

Mary was a virgin and was to marry Joseph, the carpenter. What a shock to her whole world that she would have a baby and the father would not be her future husband. How Joseph would respond and what her family and neighbors would say had to be on her mind. Mary and Joseph's wedding plans were under way, but the final steps had not been taken. Unlike today, weddings had multisteps before the ceremony was complete: First, the couple and their families would come together and exchange gifts and a groom's dowry had to be given to the bride's father. Next, there would be a ceremony at the temple—the groom leaves his house, with candles, to walk with his wedding party to the bride's house, pick up the bride, and then return to his house for the honeymoon. If Joseph did not agree, Mary's future wedding plans would have to be placed on hold. Joseph had the option to 'put her away' (Luke's gospel) or to have Mary stoned for committing adultery. What would Mary do and what would happen to her relationship with Joseph?

In Luke 1:34–35, Gabriel answered Mary's question by sharing with her that "The Holy Spirit will come upon you, and the power of the Most High will overshadow you. So the baby born to you will be holy, and he will be called the Son of God." Upon telling her that her cousin Elizabeth, who was much older and barren, was expecting a child, the angel Gabriel reassured Mary of God's power to form a baby in her virgin womb (v. 36). He appeared to answer her fears and uncertainty as to how a virgin could conceive a child. When she declared, "For nothing is impossible with God," we see Mary standing strong and filled with an unshakable resolve to be the mother of Jesus (v. 37, NLT).

Mary's favor would and did evoke the normal human reactions that are inflicted upon anyone who does something that goes against the status quo or the norm. As in Mary's day, there are still those who do not believe in the "virgin" birth. As he does throughout his writings, Luke's account of this blessed event is written in a very detailed fashion with verifiable information. We are left seeing, through Mary's miracle and other miracles in our lives today, that favor from God is both a blessing and a problem. Having favor from God may cause some people to doubt if our blessing is really from God. It can cause some people (many who have their own personal issues) to envy others who are favored because they feel that their blessing has been unfairly given to someone else. Even in the church, we have Christians who are upset that they were not selected for a particular solo, or someone "stole" their song, or someone received more recognition from the pastor than he or she did.

Indeed favor has multilayers, but it does have its benefits. What many people do not realize is that favor may cause more problems than one can even imagine. Mary had to experience the ridicule and the pain of piercing eyes and rejection because of her "favored" situation from God. Subsequently, as the only person to be with Jesus from conception to death, Mary experienced the joy and love He showed through His words and deeds. She also experienced the excruciating pain of not being able to deliver her child from the experience of carrying His own death weapon of destruction—a wooden cross. Nor could she deliver Him from His horrific death. As we live and share in the forgiveness of our sins, His pain, suffering, and resurrection are eternal hope for all humanity. In fact, Mary reminds us that because God's will and way are accomplished regardless of what stumbling blocks others may put up to try and keep God from being God, God's favor is worth whatever the world throws at us.

God's favor on Mary is not the only miracle that was pronounced by Gabriel. Her cousin Elizabeth, who was much older in age, conceived six months earlier. Elizabeth was the mother of John the Baptist, the one who would teach and preach the Good News of the Gospel and baptize Jesus in the Jordan River. Elizabeth's conception is a miracle because before God touched her womb, she could not conceive a child.

In fact, until the conception of John, Elizabeth lived with the stigma of being a barren woman. Being barren was associated with social and spiritual stigmas. The social stigmas were shame and embarrassment that God had not blessed the woman with a child. Additionally, a child provided the assurance that parents, in their old age, would be cared for.

In Mary's culture, many believed that a barren woman was disfavored by God because of some great sin she had committed. Such strong beliefs can be traced back to God's promise to Abraham that He would make him a great nation (Genesis 12:2; 15:5). Therefore, as she gave birth to a child (maybe the one to give birth to the Messiah), each woman would then be able to share in the growth of the nation (Life Application Study Bible 1996, 34).

Men were allowed to adopt a male child to be their heir and carry on their family and nation as Abraham was going to do with Eliezer, his servant, before God promised him an heir from his own loins (Genesis 15:2–3). The question begs to be asked, "Why is it that a woman is cursed because she does not have a child and provision was made for a man to have a child through adoption?"

SOMETHING TO THINK ABOUT . . .

Throughout our lives, we deal with unexpected situations that range from mild to catastrophic. Like Mary, our human response is to ask the question, "How could this have happened or why did this happen to me?" In spite of our questions or doubts, God's active presence in our lives is shown in a variety of ways. When we reflect on how the Lord has blessed us with an unanticipated blessing, we know that only God could have done that. Whether it was our rent money coming through or the healing that still baffles doctors, we know that having Jesus in our lives provides us with the faith and the hope that things will work out for the best.

Our unexpected situations that are just as intense as what Mary, Elizabeth, Joseph, and Zechariah experienced, bring feelings of emotional waves that wash through our bodies in a powerful drift. Emotions and paralyzing thoughts of being overwhelmed, in despair, shaken, broken, and despondent may overtake us. Yet, Gabriel's words to Mary from the Lord, "The Lord is with you" (Luke 1:28, NLT) are for us today. What does this mean for us when we feel hopeless and there is no light at the end of the tunnel? It means that we can lean and depend on God, who is a very present help in our times of need.

A key for us, too, today is found in the story of Mary's conception of Jesus when the incarnate Word of God became human. The gospel of John states, "And the Word was made flesh, and dwelt among us" (1:14, KJV). We should also find that the Word of God is our assurance that He will be with us; He will be in the lives of ordinary people. The Lord being with Mary is expressed in how the people around her—the relationships she had—would demonstrate the Lord with her. For example, God did not allow Mary to be alone. The relationship between Elizabeth, Zechariah, and Joseph provided assistance, comfort, and care for her.

A DOER OF THE WORD

King Solomon said, "Let us hear the conclusion of the whole matter" (Ecclesiastes 12:13, KJV). Trusting God in the unexpected requires that we really and truly have faith in a Holy God (a God without sin), who cannot and does not lie. Mary made a conscious decision to trust Him. Her faith would allow her to listen, receive, and do what the Lord had created for her life. The Lord reminded Mary and reminds us today how we can trust God in difficult and unexpected situations. Luke 1:28 (NLT) points out how God has our back and reads, "The Lord is with you." What a joy for us to hear those words and know that we can apply them to our lives as well! When we believe and live this way, life gives us responses that are rooted in God's Word.

The Lord being with us comes to life in our lives personally and collectively when we help one another. A myriad of problems in the African American community compel us to do more from the inside out for our people and all people in need. The African proverb, "It takes a village to raise a child," can be reworded to "It takes a village, or neighborhood, working together, to raise our children." In other words, we all must work together to change the destructive ripple effect in our communities. We need persons in various job capacities and at different strata in our society to lend a helping hand. In our lives, God gives us people to help us work through our challenging situations. It is up to us to learn how to engage or connect with these people for our good as well as others' good. It is up to us to take the excellence that God has placed in us, by His Spirit, and use it to trust Him in the unexpected as we follow His lead.

PRAYER

Dear Lord, thank You for our families and neighborhoods. Give us the power and wherewithal to get in the fight—to come alongside and help be a force for positive change. Then, demonstrate Your character of excellence in and through us. Amen.

IF THESE WALLS COULD TALK
(AND I BET THEY WOULD SAY SOMETHING, TOO!)

BASED ON JOSHUA 2:1–9, 12, 14–15

KEY VERSE: *"So the [two spies] set out and came to the house of a prostitute named Rahab and stayed there that night"* (Joshua 2:1, NLT).

UP FRONT AND PERSONAL

Today was the day! As we bumped along the road to the Cape Coast, there was a certain unspoken anticipation hovering in the air. A group of us had traveled from the United States to Rome and Ethiopia to Ghana. The 25-hour flight from Dulles Airport in the Washington, DC, area to Rome, Italy, to Ethiopia, Africa, and finally to Ghana, Africa, was long, draining, and exhausting. (For reasons that were never fully answered, there is not a commercial airline from Ghana that can provide a direct flight with less time from the United States to Ghana.) Yet, the much shorter bus ride from our hotel to the Cape Coast was full of emotion and anticipation about what we would soon experience during our visit to the "slave" castles.

We would have guided tours of the Dutch slave castle first and the English next. As we approached our first castle, a chilled numbness came over me as I stared out the window. The quietness inside the bus was almost stifling. It was the quietest moment I had ever experienced with this group. The silence represented to me how each person was internalizing what they might see and feel, and their anger. I could not help but wonder what really happened behind the walls of these castles. Although I cannot know the human suffering and the anguish that our ancestors went through, it is not hard to use my mind's eye to see the bodies, feel the tears, and hear the horrible cries. Putting myself in the place of someone who would be subjected to this dehumanizing existence reinforces the atrocities and pain that our ancestors suffered.

Both the Dutch and English owned and ran slave castles. These castles had dungeons—rooms with brick floors and walls that were to serve as the bedroom, the bathroom, birthing place, death bed, and meet any other basic human need that you can imagine. There were the torture dungeons where anyone who protested or fought against their enslavement or were deemed troublemakers were left to die, were killed, or were tortured. One of the most memorable experiences is the strong and stomach wrenching smell that resonates and lives within the deep brick and mortar of the Dutch slave castle. You will never forget the smell and your response to it. You cannot forget the lasting touch and the feel of the rough, dark, blood-stained, and sweat-stained bricks and mortar. You cannot forget the dashed hopes, dreams, the tears, and suffering that occurred within these walls. When I think about what our people, who were made in God's own image, must have gone through, I am humbled before God.

My life will never be the same in terms of my understanding of the events of the slave trade and the tragic and horrible conditions that were inflicted upon our ancestors. I heard what has been passed on about these conditions and some of the experiences, but I wonder what would the walls, the bricks, and mortar say if they could talk?

This study will show how God has stood with African Americans through some very hard and treacherous times. He has been our shelter, our refuge, and our hope. He has been a very present help in our times of trouble.

A WORD FROM THE LORD
SCRIPTURE: Joshua 2:1–9, 12, 14–15
PLACE: Jericho—a fortified city, surrounded by an oasis
CHARACTERS: Rahab, the two spies, Joshua

Joshua 2:1, NLT Then Joshua secretly sent out two spies from the Israelite camp at Acacia Grove. He instructed them, "Scout out the land on the other side of the Jordan River, especially around Jericho." So the two men set out and came to the house of a prostitute named Rahab and stayed there that night. **2** But someone told the king of Jericho, "Some Israelites have come here tonight to spy out the land." **3** So the king of Jericho sent orders to Rahab: "Bring out the men who have come into your house, for they have come here to spy out the whole land." **4** Rahab had hidden the two men, but she replied, "Yes, the men were here earlier, but I didn't know where they were from. **5** They left the town at dusk, as the gates were about to close. I don't know where they went. If you hurry, you can probably catch up with them." **6** (Actually, she had taken them up to the roof and hidden them beneath bundles of flax she had laid out.) **7** So the king's men went looking for the spies along the road leading to the shallow crossings of the Jordan River. And as soon as the king's men had left, the city gate of Jericho was shut. **8** Before the spies went to sleep that night, Rahab went up on the roof to talk with them. **9** "I know the LORD has given you this land," she told them. "We are all afraid of you. Everyone is living in terror.

1:12 Now swear to me by the LORD that you will be kind to me and my family since I have helped you. Give me some guarantee that

1:14 "We offer our own lives as a guarantee for your safety," the men agreed. "If you don't betray us, we will keep our promise and be kind to you when the LORD gives us the land." **15** Then, since Rahab's house was built into the town wall, she let them down by a rope through the window.

BACKGROUND
NAME: Rahab, which means "harlot," may simply mean a woman who had dealings with men
FAMILY ORIGIN: Relative of Boaz, Ruth's kinsman redeemer and husband
AGE: Unknown
MARITAL STATUS: Later became a wife
OCCUPATION: Prostitute/innkeeper
CHILDREN: Unknown
RESIDENCE: City of Jericho

NAME: Joshua, which means "Yahweh is salvation"
FAMILY ORIGIN: Father was Nun of the tribe of Ephraim (from the 12 tribes of Israel)
AGE: Over 40 when he left Egypt; over 80 when he took the leadership reigns from Moses
MARITAL STATUS: Unknown
OCCUPATION: Moses' assistant for 40 years and his successor
CHILDREN: Unknown
RESIDENCE: Egypt, the wilderness of Sinai, and Canaan (the Promised Land)

From a biblical perspective, there are three Scripture references that come to my mind and maybe yours when I hear the word *roof*. Each of these experiences involves a roof and people making life changing decisions. Here are the three Scriptures that have dynamic and altering consequences both then and now. Two of the Scriptures are found in the Old Testament: 2 Samuel 11:2 ("Rooftop Romance") and Joshua 2:6 ("Rooftop Hideaway"). The third Scripture is in the New Testament: Mark 2:4 ("A Rooftop Healing").

In each of these stories, the location is just as important as the people. From healing, to sin, to safety, the roof represents an opportunity for someone to choose to climb higher and do well or satisfy an ungodly choice. In this chapter's Scripture, we are reminded that our faith will help us to work through difficult times and to trust God.

As we examine the journey of two ex-slaves from slavery to freedom, Rahab (a converted believer), and Joshua (the new Israelite leader), there is an element of intrigue. In our present day, when spies are introduced into a story, a level of curiosity and suspense are woven into the story as well. This biblical story is no different. Questions of why and how the spies made certain decisions are left to your imagination and biblical understanding.

We begin the spy story with God's promise to the new leader, Joshua (Joshua 1:3). God promised Joshua that the land occupied by the Canaanites would belong to the Israelites. Joshua, like Moses, called for men to go look at the land that they would seize and inhabit. Unlike the 10 spies, who were apprehensive and scared of what they saw in the land and what they could not see with the hand of God, Joshua and Caleb continued on in a triumphant spirit. With the assistance of a woman named Rahab, they took risks with their lives and were able to escape capture.

As the two spies snuck into the city of Jericho, they ran for cover into Rahab's home. With Rahab's assistance, the two spies hid in or on the roof of her house (Joshua 2:6), and then ran to share their good news that the Israelites could indeed take the land (v. 24). What an interesting faith story! God does sometimes work in mysterious ways to bring us in a closer relationship with Him.

Joshua, who was Moses' successor, had been chosen by God to lead the people to the Promised Land. Joshua, whose name means "Yahweh is salvation" (Pfeiffer, Vos, and Rea 1988, 957), was prepared to use the spies' report in planning his strategy for the ultimate victory. The spies entered into Jericho, found themselves taking refuge, and hid out at a prostitute's house, named Rahab (Joshua 2:1). Some scholars, as noted in the *New International Version* of the Bible, including Josephus—the son of a priest and a great first century literary, scholarly writer on Judaism—state that Rahab was a businesswoman and an innkeeper, and *not* a prostitute (Barker, et. al.

1995, 290). Although Josephus and the Scriptures do not give the same occupational title for Rahab, they both agree that she was a very important part of the Jewish faith, particularly in the account of the two spies (Joshua 2:1; Hebrews 11:31; James 2:25).

Even though the two spies tried to work undercover, the King of Jericho knew almost immediately that they had entered the city and were staying at Rahab's home. Some of the citizens of Jericho had already informed the king (Joshua 2:2–3).

The spies left Shittim, crossed the Jordan, and then traveled another seven or eight miles to reach Jericho. It is not clear from the text how the Israelite spies stumbled or happened onto a prostitute's house for safety. Maybe they went to the prostitute's house because God led them to a place where they would not be betrayed. Or maybe because her house was the closest to the wall, the spies decided to seek refuge there. If they had chosen another house, the other good residents of Jericho may have been loyal to the king. They may have thought about how the king would protect them and their families as Rahab did by putting her trust in the Lord. Therefore, seeking refuge in Rahab's home was a lifesaving decision for the men, Rahab, and her family. The courage of all three, Rahab in particular, continues to impact our Christian lives today.

When the King's men came to Rahab's house and asked where the men were, she made a conscious decision to deceive them. Rahab had the men go to the roof and hide under the flax that she was drying on the roof (Joshua 2:6). The men could not move, sneeze, or give away their hiding spot. While the messengers from the king went searching for them, the men hid there under the cover of the night. After the messengers left, Rahab went to talk with the men and began making a deal to save her life and her family (v. 8). Rahab was not afraid to bargain for their lives. Because of what already happened to the Egyptians—the parting of the Red Sea so the ex-slaves could walk on dry land, and the utter destruction of Sihon and Og— Rahab did not want to experience any part of what God could or would do to those who were His enemies (vv. 9–11).

Rahab's quick thinking and the two spies trusting her to hide them up on the roof provided a great escape for all of them. God has a way of allowing us to trust those who are not a part of our community of faith. The Israelites had to trust who God put in their lives to bring about the Lord's plan for their present and future generations. God does choose ordinary and peculiar people to do extraordinary and peculiar work for the glory of God. Remember, look at how peculiar we are as believers and how God still loves us and works through us.

SOMETHING TO THINK ABOUT . . .

In spite of the severe roadblocks of racism, discrimination, and sexism, much was done to help the fight for Black people and help give a push for the rights of women, including White women.

As we stroll down memory lane, when we use refined sugar, we should remember Norbert Rilleaux. In the 19th century, he invented a refining machine that does the initial sugar evaporation process. From the 20th century, we should also remember Patricia Bath, who became the first African American woman doctor to receive a patent for a medical invention. She received the first patent for the eye laser machine used to remove cataracts. In addition, Colin Powell became the first African American National Security Advisor, Chairman of the Joint Chiefs of Staff, and Secretary of State. Mary Church Terrell became the first African American woman on the Washington, DC, school board. She was also cofounder of the National Association of Colored Women.

From the Buffalo Soldiers to the Tuskegee Airmen, including many unnamed women who cooked, cleaned, and worked as maids and raised other people's children and their own, African Americans have made tremendous contributions to this great country. Also included in this roll call are the countless men who were the multitalented chauffeurs and elevator operators (called "boys" by Whites), who were often their junior. Included are also jazz and blues singers/musicians from Louis Armstrong to contemporary players, and gospel singers from Thomas Dorsey to Yolanda Adams. We need to celebrate our many accomplishments and gifts that we have been given. Thank God that we have come a mighty long way; but we still have a long way to go.

As we take the time to congratulate and uplift one another for the good endeavors we see and experience for and with one another, we must remember that it is not by our own ingenuity and intellect that we have achieved. Additionally, when we think of the potential—the possibilities that are within us—there is much we need to address and conquer individually and collectively.

Life is harder for some more than for others, and the mountains of suffering can be overwhelming. Some persons wake up and decide to struggle about what outfit to wear or what to have for breakfast or lunch today. Others wake up wondering why they are still alive and if they will eat today.

Slavery, freedom, and faith are important elements that are pronounced in this amazing Old Testament. As a people, African Americans are not alienated from the pain, the fight for freedom, and victory from slavery— even the institutionalized slavery of today. When we look at facts and figures that the Legal Services for Prisoners with Children has gathered, "African Americans represent 12.7% of the U.S. population, 15% of U.S. drug users (72% of all users are White), 36.8% of those arrested for a drug-related crime, 48.2% of American adults in state and federal prisons and local jails, and 42.5% of prisoners under sentence of death" (People of Color, paragraph 1).

This information translates into the fact that "African American children (7.0%) were nearly nine times more likely to have an incarcerated parent in prison than White children (0.8%)." According to Craig Haney, Ph.D., and Philip Zimbardo, Ph.D., "the United States imprisons African American men at a rate four times greater than the rate of incarceration for Black men in South Africa" (1998, 714). An article entitled "Incarcerated America: Human Rights Watch Backgrounder" reiterates the fact that "the proportion of Blacks in prison populations exceeds the proportion among state residents in every single state. In 20 states, the percentage of Blacks incarcerated is at least five times greater than their share of resident population" (2003, paragraph 6). According to figures calculated by the U.S. Census Bureau from Census 2000 on state residents and incarcerated population, in Illinois alone "Blacks make up 15.1% of the population, but the Black percentage of incarcerated population is 62.9%. In the District of Columbia, Blacks make up 60.0% of the population, but 92.8% of those are incarcerated" (2003, Figure 2).

A DOER OF THE WORD

If these walls could talk, they would reveal that something desperately needs to be done to change these statistics, and it needs to be done now! It needs to start with more African Americans falling on their knees in prayer to a compassionate, merciful God on behalf of all humanity, and especially for their people, and rolling up their sleeves to help. It needs to start with more African Americans engaging their other brothers and sisters-in-Christ—regardless of race, creed, or color—in coming alongside and giving a hand since we are all descendants of Adam and Eve. Finally in the church, community, government, etc., since it dawned on the "powers that be" that **HIV/AIDS affects us all—it is not just a "Black thang"**—and thousands upon thousands have already died, we must never ever forget that HIV/AIDS is a very real and deadly disease for Africans and African Americans. At this writing, there is a multiracial, ethnic, and religious summit looking into how to deal with this AIDS pandemic. It is headed by prominent political and religious leaders, including Barack Obama, U.S. senator from Illinois.

We must now pray that God's Spirit *will come upon* the "powers that be"—as He did Cyrus (king of Persia), who was a pagan; he let the exiles (God's chosen people) return to Israel (Ezra 1:1). Our society should recognize putting so many of our Black men in prison, taking them from their families and communities, affects us all as well. We must pray that they not only recognize, but also do something about it.

Although we have much that we must do to make the lives of African American people healthier, spiritually grounded, educationally sound, and free from welfare dependency, we have accomplished much. Our faith in God, intelligence, hard work, laughter, tears, and caring for others has provided us with the foundation and strength we need to make a difference in the lives of others in our communities and around the world. When we think about how much our people have contributed to life and how we continue to impact so much of what is part of the life and style in the United States and around the world, we cannot help but praise God and be thankful for all that Jesus continues to do with, for, and through us in our lives.

Sometimes we can spend so much time on what we have not done and how much there is to do that we forget to pay homage and thank the Lord for the blessings that we do have. At the same time, we cannot pretend that we do not have major areas that we need to address with more than lip service or surface change. Like the spies who ran for safety to a prostitute's house and hid on the roof, we find ourselves seeking refuge in strange places with strange people. Two things we can learn from Rahab is to be careful and wise when choosing people to help us meet our needs. We sometimes choose strange and dangerous avenues for our safety, which often leads to personal death and destruction for our community. As a very colorful, smart, and exciting group of people, we sometimes forget that in the United States and around various parts of the world, we are used as a standard for how persons should look and act. We may not get paid for everything or receive the recognition, but we are very influential. Yet, because of racism, sexism, structures, and principalities that exist outside of us and what we contribute or do, we are victims and perpetrators of sin, problems, and issues that need more than just prayer. Jesus prayed and He either spoke or did something about a situation that He was responding to or creating.

When we think of all that we have accomplished through the guidance and power of God, we should always thank the Lord. From where we have been to where we are today, it is amazing! It could only be God! We must be thankful for Jesus in all that He has done, is doing, and will do in our lives and for all of God's people. We can truly testify that "Our help [is] in the name of the LORD, who made heaven and earth" (Psalm 124:8, KJV). If these walls could talk, let them proclaim that we as a Black race are living and walking in the excellence of our Lord and Savior!

PRAYER

Dear God, if these walls could talk, I pray that they would proclaim our devotion to You and Your salvation agenda—to save humanity from our sins. Help us to be instruments, or vessels, You can use to bring Your Word, hope, love, and social equality and justice to a lost and dying world. Help us to take to every needy soul the good news that the God of Israel reigns today and forevermore! Amen.

WHEN GOD SAYS, "YES"!

BASED ON ACTS 12:5–17

KEY VERSE: *"Suddenly, there was a bright light in the cell, and an angel of the Lord stood before Peter. The angel struck him on the side to awaken him and said, 'Quick! Get up!' And the chains fell off his wrists"* (Acts 12:7, NLT).

UP FRONT AND PERSONAL

It was hard to believe that this really happened. The prayer team had prayed, the church mothers had prayed, and today was the day. Each day D. King dreaded going to the mailbox and taking out the mail. Both he and his wife, Debbie, worked, but their money always seemed shorter than the month and the bills they had to pay. The bills and the usual junk mail were present to encourage them to make more bills. His father, who had been a postman for years (most mail handlers in Washington, DC, are Black), told him to always open his mail because you never know what could be inside. Since the scare of anthrax and mail bombs, he had to modify what his father said.

On this much anticipated day, the mail came and everything looked like junk mail or bills. In fact, a letter from the church, the "begging" mail as the church persons whispered behind the pastor's back, had arrived. D. King threw the mail on the table and began preparing himself a sandwich. Things were more than tight and his anxiety and frustration with God were growing.

Did God not hear my prayers over the last few months, weeks, days, and now to every minute? he asked himself. *What is God doing?*

Yes, he had spent money gambling, but he joined the local GA (Gamblers Anonymous) and life was better. His kids were doing well, his wife was easier to live with these days, and even his nosy neighbors were relieved that the number of cars and people coming and going from his house had subsided. As he retired for bed, his wife, Debbie, who had come home from one of those long, drawn out church board meetings, asked if the mail had come. He replied, "Yes." She could tell by his response that the Lord had not answered their prayers.

She thought about how they had learned to pray together and how their marriage was stronger. Her spirit was down and she wondered why God had not addressed their prayers. Debbie believed in prayer, but was quite disappointed that God had not helped them out. Before she climbed into bed, Debbie asked her husband, "Where is the mail?" He told her that it was on the table.

She went to get the mail and discovered that he was right; only junk mail and bills were there. But then she, too, remembered what her father-in-law said to her husband, "Always open your mail. You never know what is inside." (He would also always add, "If there is no return address, it is best to leave it alone.")

Debbie decided to open all the mail and look at the bills and see if there was any good junk mail to read. The first bill, in the pink envelope, was for $325.00, and needed to be paid to the electric company as soon as possible. Yet, when Debbie read the next bill, she realized it was not a bill at all. Her heart leaped with joy and her eyes filled with tears as she read the bold black letters: "Since we received your medical insurance payment from the company, a credit of $1,000 has been issued to your account for the payment that you personally made. A check for this amount is attached below." Debbie cried silent tears of joy and whispered a prayer of "thank You" to Jesus for helping them through this difficult time.

Sometimes the answers to prayers are like what God asked Moses, "What is that in your hand?" (Exodus 4:2, NLT).

A WORD FROM THE LORD
SCRIPTURE: Acts 12:5–17
PLACE: Jerusalem
CHARACTER: Peter

Acts 12:5, NLT But while Peter was in prison, the church prayed very earnestly for him. **6** The night before Peter was to be placed on trial, he was asleep, fastened with two chains between two soldiers. Others stood guard at the prison gate. **7** Suddenly, there was a bright light in the cell, and an angel of the Lord stood before Peter. The angel struck him on the side to awaken him and said, "Quick! Get up!" And the chains fell off his wrists. **8** Then the angel told him, "Get dressed and put on your sandals." And he did. "Now put on your coat and follow me," the angel ordered. **9** So Peter left the cell, following the angel. But all the time he thought it was a vision. He didn't realize it was actually happening. **10** They passed the first and second guard posts and came to the iron gate leading to the city, and this opened for them all by itself. So they passed through and started walking down the street, and then the angel suddenly left him. **11** Peter finally came to his senses. "It's really true!" he said. "The Lord has sent his angel and saved me from Herod and from what the Jewish leaders had planned to do to me!" **12** When he realized this, he went to the home of Mary, the mother of John Mark, where many were gathered for prayer. **13** He knocked at the door in the gate, and a servant girl named Rhoda came to open it. **14** When she recognized Peter's voice, she was so overjoyed that, instead of opening the door, she ran back inside and told everyone, "Peter is standing at the door!" **15** "You're out of your mind!" they said. When she insisted, they decided, "It must be his angel." **16** Meanwhile, Peter continued knocking. When they finally opened the door and saw him, they were amazed. **17** He motioned for them to quiet down and told them how the Lord had led him out of prison. "Tell James and the other brothers what happened," he said. And then he went to another place.

BACKGROUND

NAME: Peter (Simeon; Simon; Cephas [Jesus gave him the name, 'The Rock'])
FAMILY ORIGIN: brother, Andrew, who was also a disciple
AGE: Unknown
MARITAL STATUS: Married
OCCUPATION: Fisherman, disciple, notable apostle
CHILDREN: Unknown
RESIDENCE: original home was Bethsaida, which was a fishing village on the northern shore of the Sea of Galilee, not far from Capernaum (John 1:44; Pfeiffer, Vos, and Rea 1988, 1317). He also resided in Jerusalem and outside of Jerusalem (1988, 1319).

Herod, who had James—the brother of John—put to death with a sword (Acts 12:2), decided to continue his rampage and destructive acts by harassing Peter. Now Herod did not think of causing grief in Peter's life all by himself. He had been encouraged by the Jewish people's response to what he did to James. Therefore, Peter found himself locked up in jail. Peter's prison sentence was during the Feast of the Unleavened Bread or Passover. This feast was a time for the Jews to eat no leaven (yeast) bread. It was not allowed, and their specific meal began at twilight on the 14th of Nisan (Leviticus 23:4–5), and the week following the Passover meal. Both names became interchangeable by the New Testament time (Barker, et. al. 1995, 1579). Nisan is "the first month of the Jewish calendar (Nehemiah 2:1; Esther 3:7), called Abib in the Pentateuch. It denoted the month of flowers during which the Passover occurred and corresponds to our March and April" (Pfeiffer, Vos, and Rea 1988, 1210).

In Acts 12:4, after Passover, Herod gave Peter over to the four squads of four soldiers and they brought Peter to a public trial. There was "one company of four soldiers for each of the four watches of the night" (Barker, et. al. 1995, 1670). "But while Peter was in prison the church prayed very earnestly for him. The night before Peter was to be placed on trial, he was asleep, fastened with two chains between two soldiers. Others stood guard at the prison gate" (Acts 12:5–6, NLT). The Scriptures do not tell us if Peter prayed for himself, but we do know that the Lord sent an angel to free Peter.

Have you noticed that God sometimes begins something new by working through the side of someone (i.e., with Adam, a rib was taken from his side to begin a new life—Eve; or when Jesus had a sword thrust into his side on the Cross to end life, which was a new beginning for all life)?

The angel hurried Peter to put on his clothes, his sandals, and his coat and start walking out of the prison. Peter, who had been asleep, believed that he was not experiencing reality. As Peter walked through the prison toward freedom, he still had not fully grasped that God had set him free.

With the angel, Peter walked past the watchful eyes of the guards. No one noticed him or the angel. Eventually, both Peter and the angel came to the iron gate of the city and a miracle happened—the gate opened up by itself and they walked through. Finally, the angel left Peter and he was fully awake. Peter did not hesitate to acknowledge what the Lord had done to deliver him from Herod, and what some of the Jewish people hoped would happen to him (Acts 12:10–11).

After giving God the victory and accepting his newfound freedom, Peter went to the home of Mary, the mother of John Mark, who is also considered to be the author of the gospel of Mark. He interpreted for Peter, and traveled with Paul and Barnabas. Mary is also the sister of Barnabas.

Mary's home has been noted by some scholars as the possible home for the Last Supper or Passover meal. If this is so, then Mary or some of her servants may have served Jesus and the disciples the Last Supper. Maybe Mary or one of the women could have been in the background when Jesus talked to the disciples about who would betray them. This is a thought to consider only because the men would not have been cooking at the home of a wealthy woman who had servants. The women had been cooking and preparing food for Jesus and the disciples before this time, so maybe the women were there (N.S. 2003, 15).

Peter knocked on the outer door and a young woman named Rhoda, who was a servant, opened the door. The outer door signifies that the home is of someone with wealth (Coogan, et. al. 2001, 207). A servant answering the door lets us know that Mary was a woman with financial status (Acts 12:13–14).

While the prayer team gathered and prayed for Peter, he was standing at the door and knocking to come in. Rhoda, the servant, heard the knock and heard Peter's voice as he was standing at the gate; but she was too excited to open the gate. Instead she ran back inside to tell everyone the good news. They did not believe her. They even told her that she had lost her mind, but Rhoda insisted that she was right (Acts 12:14–15). Peter kept knocking. His persistent knock was not heard by the others because they were debating whether it was him. In their disbelief of what God had done, they were still not able to comprehend that a mighty man of God had been released from jail by the same all-powerful God that they were praying to. It must not have been Peter at the gate, but "his angel" they proclaimed (v. 15). It was believed that a person's guardian angel resembled the "person being protected" (Coogan, et. al. 2001, 207). God is a miracle worker!

Finally, they decided to investigate Rhoda's miracle story for themselves (Acts 12:16). To his friends' surprise (and maybe his family's also), Peter, and not his angel, was standing at the gate (v. 16). He quieted and calmed them down so that he could share his amazing deliverance story with them.

After sharing the story, Peter told them to let James, Jesus' brother, and the other brothers know what had happened (Acts 12:17). Jesus' brother, James, had become the new leader of the Jerusalem church (Galatians 15:13, 19; 2:12). Peter left to tell others about the miracle that had happened.

God said, "Yes" to the prayers of the church, but the people could not believe that the Lord had answered so quickly and without any trouble or problems for Peter. What a miracle and a mighty blessing!

SOMETHING TO THINK ABOUT . . .

Often we find ourselves wanting God to say, "Yes," but we do not fully accept God's 'yes.' We either think that we are dreaming; we are too excited to act responsively right away; or we do not believe, and we doubt that the Lord did what He said He would do.

Why do we respond slowly, or do not believe God will do what He says, or even believe that He will give us a special blessing that we could never have thought of ourselves? We often forget that there is power in prayer. Prayer changes our expectations, and keeps bringing us into a trusting relationship with the Lord.

Peter's church family prayed, but they did not believe God would act in such a hurry. God's quick "yes" is sometimes a surprise to us as well.

Even today, God has a peculiar way of showing up and not doing things as we think they should be done. For example, why is it that some people can get away with all kinds of things, but as soon you do something that is not considered "good" Christian behavior or thinking, you are punished? Some people do receive God's "favor" or "pardon" more than others, or at least during those crucial life and death moments. How many times do we witness individuals receiving money, lavish gifts, job promotions, the special husband or wife, disciplined children (not bebe kids), church position, community status, and good friends, and we wonder why God won't give us another chance or give us that kind of blessing?

Throughout the Bible, we see that often when Jesus saved an individual, He did not always give everyone his/her particular heart's desire. There were various reasons. We also find that being honest with self and the Lord are very important. In fact, strong consequences often occur when a person's heart's desire was in disobedience to what Jesus expected from him/her. Doing things our way and not God's way can be costly and sometimes deadly. The cost and death can be reflected in nonproducing ministries, relationships, and physical and emotional death, which we may never be resurrected from in this life. Trying to outsmart God always results in our being in the lesser weight category and our arms being too short to box with God.

After we pray, what is our action or response? Sometimes we are to wait, but many times we need to act. We pray that we will have cleaner and better communities; but when was the last time you heard or saw a national push for cleaning up our streets on a monthly basis to give us a litter-free community and no more boarded up houses?

Responding to God's "yes," in a positive way, requires discipline and a willingness to trust God. God's "yes" is not always swift, but it will come in God's timing. For instance, the Hebrews prayed for deliverance during the more than 400 years they were in slavery in Egypt. Black people prayed for deliverance as well for the more than 200 years they were in slavery in the United States. God's answer to both prayers was "yes, but not now."

God sent Moses to deliver the Hebrew people from slavery. In 1865, it took several slave revolts, anti-slavery protests, and a Civil War before Black people were freed from legal chattel slavery. On a national level, the Emancipation Proclamation of January 1, 1863, was the first act to abolish slavery (Smith and Palmisano 2000, 874).

This historic and new freedom has been thought of as the reason for the Watch Night Service, or Freedom's Eve, which has been celebrated in African American churches over the years. Enslaved Africans had gathered for many years on December 31 to spend time together because the slave owners "tallied up their business accounts on the first day of each new year. Human property was sold along with land and furnishings to satisfy debts" (Sutton 2004, paragraph 4). If their family members and friends were sold, they would probably not see each other again, so the time of celebration at the end of the year was important (2004, paragraph 4).

The highly anticipated Emancipation Proclamation was an added part of the celebration on December 31, 1862. The slaves and the freed Africans anxiously awaited the news that Lincoln's signed word would become a reality. As the slaves waited for the news on January 1, 1863, they were able to rejoice that the promise was true when they received word later in the day. Although the Confederate states received word of this on January 1, 1863, the state of Texas did not legally set the slaves free until June 17th of that same year. We celebrate this as Juneteenth to commemorate the freedom of the slaves from Texas.

Watch Night Service indeed was a time to celebrate and give thanks. Slavery and the horrendous Middle Passage caused the deaths of thousands of Africans who were either thrown overboard because they died on the ship, or—as we have been taught—jumped to escape slavery. Many scholars have discovered what might have happened from folklore tales "that emphasized joining forces with their ancestors to defeat their European captives" (Smith and Palmisano 2000, 964). When God responds with a slow "yes" in our lives, how do we respond?

A DOER OF THE WORD

God's "yes" in our lives should cause us to respond in discipline and with a willing heart to do what the Lord has set before us in our relationships. Discipline in our lives is necessary. Discipline and obedience require us to make certain lifestyle changes. It also requires us to have a willingness to make choices that move us beyond our comfort zone. This move will help us get over our defeatist attitudes and actions. It is amazing that we would rather choose to live in denial and lie about the present. We see evidence of this not only in our social issues from drugs to relationships, but also in how we respond to what the Lord requires of us.

God expects us to care for one another. The Bible is replete with stories demonstrating that the Lord wants us to share compassion and love with one another. Micah 6:8 (KJV) poses the question with the answer already in the question, "What doth the LORD require of thee, but to do justly, and to love mercy, and to walk humbly with thy God?" There are times that we would rather not care for one another at the expense of keeping what we think should be ours. We worked for it, whatever it is, and no one else should have any claims to it. Jesus wants us to say, "Yes" to His Word and follow in His way and in our selflessness.

The power of prayer and our response are very much a part of our lives as Christians. We do know that sometimes God does not always respond to our prayers with "yes." Sometimes He responds with "no" or "later." Learning to wait for God's response can be very difficult and hard to do. Waiting can be extremely uncomfortable and tearful. Yet, the more we trust in Jesus, the stronger we grow in our faith.

What a blessing and a joy for us to experience God responding to our prayers with "yes," "no," or "later." God communicates to us, and how we communicate back to the Lord provides definition to our faith. Prayer is power and gives us hope for today and tomorrow. Prayer helps us to move toward excellence in our walk with a Holy God.

PRAYER

Lord, thank You for the many times that Your answer to our prayers is "yes"! We pray, however, that when Your answer is "no" or "later" that You will give us the patience and fortitude to wait on You, because You always know what is best for us and have our best interest at heart! Amen.

AFRAID, BUT NOT ALONE

BASED ON JUDGES 4:4–16

KEY VERSE: *"Then Deborah said to Barak, 'Get ready! This is the day the LORD will give you victory over Sisera, for the LORD is marching ahead of you.' So Barak led his 10,000 warriors down the slopes of Mount Tabor into battle"* (Judges 4:14, NLT).

UP FRONT AND PERSONAL

Flashback: Think of a time when you were afraid and needed someone to give you encouragement and support to make a decision or do the right thing. Here is a story to help us think about how fear has stopped us and what we could have done to assist others in their fears. It is always easier to help someone when we are not involved, and 20/20 hindsight always seems better in solving issues.

"What would she do?" Carmen knew that she had to make a decision that would affect her life now and forevermore. She had been offered and accepted a full, four-year scholarship to prestigious Spelman College in Atlanta, Georgia. She already started a summer program at Spelman that was exciting, challenging, and hard.

The students in the summer program complained about the workload, but everyone was looking forward to classes—or so they thought. Carmen had also been offered an entry-level job with promotional opportunities to a high-level manager's position and salaries to match. She was going back and forth in her mind about what to do.

Carmen was nervous about taking a job, but she needed the money—her family needed the money. The job gave her the opportunity to make the money she needed in the field she wanted, and she had the potential to quickly move up the corporate ladder. Carmen had a deadline date of one week to accept the job. The company really wanted her and the school did not want her to leave.

The week seemed too short and Carmen became ill for a few days. Fear of the unknown had overtaken her decision making process. The pressure from her family was growing and her new friends encouraged her to stay at school. Because she felt a heavy weight on her to care for the family, Carmen was afraid to stay at school. Her dream to complete college was becoming a tearful and painful distant dream. She needed help and quickly.

Carmen talked to her grandmother, and her grandmother also wanted her to continue in school; but she knew that the family needed Carmen immediately to assist. Another dream deferred, her grandmother thought, so she prayed that Carmen would be able to attend school and provide the financial and emotional support the family needed.

They were a praying family, and they expected the Lord to work things out. Yet, they depended on young Carmen to bail them out. The job was certain, but the school offered an unknown. She would rather live in the unknown, but Carmen made her decision and turned to Corporate America to help her family. As she looked back at the school one last time, a single tear gently and slowly rolled down her face. She knew in her heart that she would never come back, but only hoped that one day she could go back to school.

A WORD FROM THE LORD
SCRIPTURE: Judges 4:4–16
PLACE: Canaan (Israel)
CHARACTERS: Deborah and Barak

Judges 4:4, NLT Deborah, the wife of Lappidoth, was a prophet who had become a judge in Israel. **5** She would hold court under the Palm of Deborah, which stood between Ramah and Bethel in the hill country of Ephraim, and the Israelites came to her to settle their disputes. **6** One day she sent for Barak son of Abinoam, who lived in Kedesh in the land of Naphtali. She said to him, "This is what the LORD, the God of Israel, commands you: Assemble ten thousand warriors from the tribes of Naphtali and Zebulun at Mount Tabor. **7** I will lure Sisera, commander of Jabin's army, along with his chariots and warriors, to the Kishon River. There I will give you victory over him." **8** Barak told her, "I will go, but only if you go with me!" **9** "Very well," she replied, "I will go with you. But since you have made this choice, you will receive no honor. For the LORD's victory over Sisera will be at the hands of a woman." So Deborah went with Barak to Kedesh. **10** At Kedesh, Barak called together the tribes of Zebulun and Naphtali, and ten thousand warriors marched up with him.

Deborah also marched with them. **11** Now Heber the Kenite, a descendant of Moses' brother-in-law Hobab, had moved away from the other members of his tribe and pitched his tent by the Oak of Zaanannim, near Kedesh. **12** When Sisera was told that Barak son of Abinoam had gone up to Mount Tabor, **13** he called for all nine hundred of his iron chariots and all of his warriors, and they marched from Harosheth-haggoyim to the Kishon River. **14** Then Deborah said to Barak, "Get ready! Today the LORD will give you victory over Sisera, for the LORD is marching ahead of you." So Barak led his ten thousand warriors down the slopes of Mount Tabor into battle. **15** When Barak attacked, the LORD threw Sisera and all his charioteers and warriors into a panic. Then Sisera leaped down from his chariot and escaped on foot. **16** Barak chased the enemy and their chariots all the way to Harosheth-haggoyim, killing all of Sisera's warriors. Not a single one was left alive.

BACKGROUND
NAME: Deborah*
FAMILY ORIGIN: from the tribe of Joseph (one of Jacob's [Israel's] 12 sons)
AGE: Unknown
MARITAL STATUS: Married to Lappidoth
OCCUPATION: Prophetess and Judge
CHILDREN: Unknown
RESIDENCE: Canaan
*Deborah was the fourth and only female judge of Israel and had special abilities as an adviser, counselor, and a mediator (Life Application Study Bible 1996, 359).

NAME: Barak, whose name means "thunderbolt"
FAMILY ORIGIN: from the tribe of Naphtali (one of the 12 tribes of Israel)
AGE: Unknown
MARITAL STATUS: Unknown
OCCUPATION: a military leader encouraged by the judge and prophetess Deborah to deliver the northern tribes of Israel from bondage imposed by King Jabin, the king of Hazor. King Jabin had 900 chariots of iron, and an Egyptian or a Hittite named Sisera led his army. "He [Barak] was called upon to gather an army from Zebulun and Naphtali" (Pfeiffer, Vos, and

Rea 1988, 204).
CHILDREN: Unknown
RESIDENCE: Ephraim

Deborah was one of the greatest judges of Israel. She was known for her leadership as a judge over Israel, and also for having the distinct honor of being the only judge who God selected as a prophetess as well. What an honor from God! The Lord gave Deborah the high privilege to have the character and the stamina to serve double duty—a judge and a prophetess. In addition to being a judge and a prophetess, Deborah was married to Lappidoth.

Deborah called for the military leader, Barak, to follow God's command for him to go and defeat Sisera and his troops. Barak, whose name means "thunderbolt," is the commander for Israel's army (Judges 4:4–7). He obviously had the skill and the military fortitude to lead, do, and conquer. Plotting, planning, and executing orders were not new to Barak. So when Deborah sent for Barak and shared with him what the Lord had spoken to her for Barak to do, his response was somewhat surprising. Deborah laid out the Lord's plan to Barak with the assurance of victory. Using his military training, all Barak needed to do was to follow God's plan and win the battle. But an odd thing happened to Barak. This "mighty" soldier was not willing to accept his already won assignment.

We see in Judges 4:8 that Barak gave a conditional response to Deborah's word to fight and claim the victory. Barak said to her, "If you will go with me, I will go; but if you don't go with me, I won't go." Without Deborah, he was sure that he would not and could not go and fight.

Deborah responded to his fear in a clear and firm message. She did not give up on him, talk about him in a negative way, or say that she would find someone else to carry out God's plan. No. Deborah agreed to go with Barak (Judges 4:9). She informed him that the "honor will be yours [Barak], for the Lord will hand Sisera over to a woman" (v. 21). As already stated in the original command from God, Deborah went with Barak into battle along with ten thousand men from Zebulum and Naphtali (4:6). Barak was ready to go into battle, so he moved into position to fight with his ten thousand men and took Judge Deborah with him.

Before battle, it is not usual for warriors to send spies to spy out the land. Not doing so could cause soldiers, in the heat of battle, to become "turncoats," who watch, plot, and reveal the plans to the enemy. As Barak and his forces went up to Mount Tabor (v. 12), we discover that Heber, a Kenite, was watching Barak and his movements. In Judges 4:10–11, we see that Heber, who had traveled with the other Kenites, and was related to Moses through marriage, actually pitched a tent by the "great tree in Zaanannim." The text informs us that Heber belonged to the Kenite people. His identity as a Kenite indicates that the members of his clan were metalworkers and they probably had been in close relationship with Israel from Moses time (Barker, et. al. 1995, 332).

According to Judges 4:7, Sisera, who had mighty chariots of war, had already planned on how he would fight. The plan was indeed great from a military vantage point, but God's plan was and is always better and victorious. As scholars have noted, Sisera's plan to fight along the Kishon River would give his chariots ample space to move, but Sisera did not plan on God being involved in the fighting. He either forgot or did not know how the Lord had defeated the Egyptians at the Red Sea, Og and Sihon, and Joshua's battles of victory from the Lord, which included a hailstorm from heaven. Sisera was no match for God's military genius.

In Judges 4:14, Deborah told Barak to go and fight. She even reminded him that God had already given him the victory. Barak's fear was no longer a dominant factor for who should go into battle with him. He was now ready and willing to fight and to win. Barak descended Mount Tabor with his ten thousand men behind him. In verse 15, something unexpected and amazing happened as Barak went forward to fight. The Lord caused Sisera's men to become afraid or panic. The verse states that "the LORD routed Sisera and all his chariots and army by the sword" (NIV). Sisera, who immediately saw that he could not win nor did he have backup to help him fight, took off running.

We often hear how "the captain" should stay with the troops or on the ship even if the battle or ship is sinking, but life preservation tends to win out over our admirable thoughts. Consequently, Sisera took off running while Barak and his men killed all the enemy soldiers that were left on the battlefield. Barak represents "other warriors of Israel who lacked trust in God" (Barker, et. al. 1995, 332).

SOMETHING TO THINK ABOUT . . .

In Bible history, it was a disgrace for a soldier to be killed by a woman

(Barker, et. al. 1995, 343). Even today, the shame or stigma of a boy or a man being conquered in any particular areas by a girl or woman can bring dishonor and a feeling of being inadequate. For example, in the movie *Akeelah and the Bee* (Lions Gate 2006), the competition for the National Spelling Bee comes down to a girl and a boy. The boy's father emphasizes to his son that he should not let a girl beat him.

It is quite sobering to realize that no matter how much education you may have, how much physical dexterity you possess, how much material goods you have accumulated, or how much business savvy you have acquired, fear can humble you to your knees. In fact when fear visits us and is allowed to reside within our hearts, it can reduce us to a weak servant that trembles and quakes with every step. Fear is a wake-up call to us that we are not invincible and that we do not have all power in our hands.

There are times when fear serves as a positive factor in our lives—a warning sign that danger or a problem is close at hand. Unfortunately, fear also carries stinging rays that shoot darts of lethal proportions. These darts can immobilize us and keep us from thinking rationally and acting responsibly and compassionately when we need to. Fear can also keep us focused on what we *cannot* do or see, rather than on an all-knowing, all-present, and all-powerful God.

A DOER OF THE WORD

When we embrace fear and allow it to be our guide, we feel alone, desolate, forgotten, and hopeless. These feelings are transformed into actions that support our internal feelings, which have been generated from fear. Instead of responding with "I am speaking out and standing up for my rights or the rights of others," we physically slouch, withdraw from the engagement, and use a myriad of mental gymnastics called "excuses" to keep us from doing what shows boldness and courage.

Fear is not limited to a particular person, place, or time. The domination of fear in our lives is demonstrated in numerous ways. A very prominent fear factor in our society is racism and its cousins: sexism and economic exploitation. In has been woven as one of the many narcissistic fibers that are a part of the foundation of the United States.

As we strive for excellence in our Christian walk, we need to recognize that fear is a timeless and patient aspect of our humanity that encourages us *not* to trust God, but lean or take refuge in our own thoughts or the enticing words of others. Fear is not a stranger to people. However, it often serves as a strong inner character reference that we depend on. Sadly, it keeps us from fully developing our intimate relationship with Jesus. It keeps us from graduating to spiritual greatness.

PRAYER

Father God, help us to manage our fears and keep them in their proper perspective. May we always know that You do not give us "the spirit of fear; but of power, and of love, and of a sound mind" (2 Timothy 1:7, KJV). Amen.

JESUS IN STRANGE PLACES

BASED ON LUKE 19:1–10

KEY VERSE: *"Jesus responded, 'Salvation has come to this home today, for this man has shown himself to be a true son of Abraham'"* (Luke 19:9, NLT).

UP FRONT AND PERSONAL

Michael Yaconelli said in his book *Messy Spirituality,* "It's difficult to be odd in a culture of sameness. Society is not kind to the *odd, strange, the different, the broken, and the rejects*" (2002, 84). It is difficult to be odd in a culture that values sameness and applauds people who say, "I do not look at the color of someone's skin." Taking advantage of someone who is the "underdog" is not limited to a particular race, religious belief, or gender. Research shows that rich people take advantage of the poor and middle-class people around the world. Countries that have less economic and literal fire power are held hostage to economic and military sanctions that the countries of power hold to be true and dear for themselves. How is it that during WWII, the atomic bomb could be dropped on people of color, but not on anyone in Europe or Russia?

At some point, most people cannot help but see the physical differences of those we encounter. Even if a person is blind, he or she will ask someone who can see to describe what the person looks like.

There was once a minister who was blind. He had the definite gift of good wit and a great sense of humor. He had a warm personality and knew how to make a person feel welcome and comfortable. Let us call him "Reverend Brown." He was the type of person who could compliment you on what you were wearing and could tap into what you were feeling by a handshake or what you said.

He could tap into someone's inner thoughts through a handshake or their words, and it was baffling how he knew what that person was wearing. One day, a close friend asked him if he had someone else to describe the interested person to him. He only laughed and said, "I have the gift."

This friend later found out that the good Reverend had the gift of finding someone that he could trust. He would then stand near someone who would share with him who was in the room, what he/she wore, and if anything in particular stood out about the person. The gift he had was the ability to memorize, internalize the information, and share with the individual his or her own personal information. His understanding that he was different and that being independent meant that he had to learn, know, process, and understand quickly was crucial to his surviving and enjoying life in ways that many seeing people cannot imagine.

God loves *imperfect* people. If we think about the myriad of people that God worked through in the Old Testament alone, we know that God's love is not for those who are perfect and loving at all times. For example, think of some of the more notable individuals that God chose to do a great work for his people and God's glory: Moses, who was a murderer and a leader; David, who was an adulterer, murderer, and leader; and Rahab, who was possibly a temple prostitute, liar, or an innkeeper. As we travel through the New Testament, we also see again and again how God loves imperfect people. In the New Testament, He loves them through Jesus Christ.

We see Peter, who was a coward, courageous, great with a sword, and a disciple; Paul, who was a conspirator to murder, abusive and cruel to Christians, and a devout follower of Christ; and Mary, who was a prostitute and foot washer, with tears and hair, for Jesus.

God does love imperfect people, but not our behavior and thoughts that are demoralizing and degrading to others and self. In fact, God wants us to change our actions and hearts so that we can share the love of God through Christ Jesus.

A WORD FROM THE LORD
SCRIPTURE: Luke 19:1–10
PLACE: Jericho
CHARACTER: Zacchaeus

Luke 19:1, NLT Jesus entered Jericho and made his way through the town. **2** There was a man there named Zacchaeus. He was the chief tax collector in the region, and he had become very rich. **3** He tried to get a look at Jesus, but he was too short to see over the crowd. **4** So he ran ahead and climbed a sycamore-fig tree beside the road, for Jesus was going to pass that way. **5** When Jesus came by, he looked up at Zacchaeus and called him by name. "Zacchaeus!" he said. "Quick, come down! I must be a guest in your home today." **6** Zacchaeus quickly climbed down and took Jesus to his house in great excitement and joy. **7** But the crowds were displeased. "He has gone to be the guest of a notorious sinner," they grumbled. **8** Meanwhile, Zacchaeus stood before the Lord and said, "I will give half my wealth to the poor, Lord, and if I have cheated people on their taxes, I will give them back four times as much!" **9** Jesus responded, "Salvation has come to this home today, for this man has shown himself to be a true son of Abraham. **10** For the Son of Man came to seek and save those who are lost."

BACKGROUND
NAME: Zacchaeus
FAMILY ORIGIN: in the Abrahamic line (Luke 19:9)
AGE: Unknown
MARITAL STATUS: Unknown
OCCUPATION: 'Chief tax collector—only noted here in the Bible—possibly means one in charge of a district, with other tax collectors under him (money maker)' (Pfeiffer, Vos, Rea 1988, 1831). It is like programs today where you have a representative who then recruits other representatives—known for his short height, change of heart, and way of living.
CHILDREN: Unknown
RESIDENCE: Jericho

NAME: the Crowd—the usual group of complainers who did not like who Jesus hung out with
PROP: the Sycamore-fig Tree—"sturdy tree, 30–40 feet high, with a short trunk and spreading branches—can hold a grown man" (Barker, et. al. 1995, XXX).

The story of Zacchaeus is usually told about a short man who climbed up in a tree to see Jesus. As Jesus was walking through the city, he noticed Zacchaeus and called him down from the tree. Zacchaeus responded to Jesus' invitation and invited him to dinner. The crowd complained about Jesus' dinner company choice. This, of course, did not discourage Jesus or Zacchaeus. A transformation took place within Zacchaeus and he had a new attitude that transformed his past business practices and his heart.

Jesus received Zacchaeus and welcomed him into the family of God.

A brief summary of this incident gives us an overview, but does not allow us to enter into the details of the story. Let us share together what the gospel writer, Luke, speaks to us in the text and for us today.

Luke begins this story with Jesus in one of his usual modes of transportation when something different is about to happen in the life or the lives of others. Jesus was walking through the city of Jericho (Luke 19:1). Luke begins by telling us that He (Jesus) was going into the city, but He was apparently not planning to have any layover time there. Yet, Jesus' walking signals to us that a transforming event was about to happen. For example, when He walked to see the woman at the well, new living water was discovered (John 4). When Jesus began his disciple's recruitment program, He walked to call some working fishermen by the names of Peter, James, and John. As Jesus walked into the town, He noticed that there was a man sitting up in the tree. There were plenty of other people around, but this particular man caught his attention. Jesus saw Zacchaeus and called for him to climb down from out of the tree (Luke 19:1–5). Why would Zacchaeus, a tax collector, climb up in a tree to see Jesus?

Taxes on the Jewish citizens had been imposed by the ruling Roman government. Therefore, the Jews, who were subject to the Romans, put tax collectors in the same category as a sinner. The word *sinner* referred to anyone who did not "follow the Mosaic Law, as interpreted by the teachers of the law," or who was considered evil (Mark 2:14; Barker, et. al. 1995, 1494).

Zacchaeus was a wealthy tax collector, as were other tax collectors during this time. Levi, whose name was changed to Matthew, and one of the 12 disciples' of Christ, was employed as a tax collector before he became a disciple of Jesus. The tax collectors would be in their toll booths, on a "major international road," collecting taxes as people traveled from "Damascus through Capernaum to the Mediterranean Coast and to Egypt" (Barker, et. al. 1995, 1494).

Jericho was an important city. Located in the Jordan Valley approximately eight miles northwest of the Jordan River, it was "the most ancient instance of urban civilization known to man," and it "flourished as a fortified city" (Pfeiffer, Vos, and Rea 1988, 900). Zacchaeus worked in this busy city that was a "customs center" for the Roman government by collecting the taxes from the people. Many people would be passing through Jericho traveling to other destinations for business or other purposes, so the profit made by the tax collectors was at a high premium. The tax collectors could charge double or more in taxes and keep the excess for themselves. However, they had to make sure that the Roman government received what they were expecting to be paid. Zacchaeus obviously had charged the people more than enough and conspired with the government to collect the money, which represented the Roman power in the land. His line of work was very much disliked by the people; therefore, they resented that Jesus would even want to eat with him—"To eat with a person was a sign of friendship" (Barker, et. al. 1995, 1494; Mark 2:15). Consequently, they grumbled and complained when Jesus told Zacchaeus that he wanted to stay at his house today (Luke 19:5). Verse 5 tells us that Jesus' invitation "is considered a divine necessity" (Barker, et. al. 1995, 1574).

The joy that Zacchaeus felt was evidenced by how he responded to Jesus' invitation. The fact that Jesus would invite Himself to Zacchaeus' house was indeed amazing. In spite of the people's noises and their remark that Jesus "has gone to be the guest of one who is a sinner," Zacchaeus was delighted (Luke 19:7). His new lease on life was evidenced in how he decided to change his life around. Although the naysayers had a right to complain, did you notice that no one complained or sounded excited that Zacchaeus was a new man? Maybe they could not believe that such a man could change and give up his money as well? In verse 8, his "vow amounting to repentance" is demonstrated in the amount of money. "Four times" he will pay back to those he had overtaxed (Coogan, et. al. 2001, 133). This is an overabundance of what he had taken and shows that he has changed. The money is no longer the object of love. The quadruple payment is also noted as the "extreme repayment required under the law in case of theft" (Barker, et. al. 1995, 1574; Exodus 22:1; 2 Samuel 12:6 c.f.; Proverbs 6:31).

In verses 9 and 10, two key phrases are used by Jesus when He spoke to Zacchaeus again. The first phrase is "son of Abraham" and His second phrase is "Son of Man." Jesus tells Zacchaeus that he was in the 'lineage of Abraham. . .and one who walks "in the footsteps" of Abraham's faith (Romans 4:12), even though the Jewish society excluded him" (Barker, et. al. 1995, 1574). What a marvelous reception for Zacchaeus, who had experienced hurting others and wanting to restore what he had taken! He is restored and welcomed back into the family.

The second phrase, "Son of Man," is important and is used in the gospel of Luke, throughout the gospels, Acts, and the book of Revelation. It gives a summary of Jesus' purpose—to bring salvation, meaning, eternal life (Luke 18:18), and the kingdom of God (v. 25).

Zacchaeus' decision to give back money to those he had cheated is in contrast to the rich young ruler's reply to Jesus in the previous chapter (Luke 18:18–25). Zacchaeus' change in heart affected his attitude about life and how he treated others. His new way of thinking gave him a gracious and effective way to live his life and care for others. Zacchaeus became a man of compassion and integrity. He became a man who lived and walked in the excellence of Jesus.

SOMETHING TO THINK ABOUT . . .

We enjoy reading stories with happy endings, but what about the stories of children and adults who are considered odd, weak, or vulnerable and experience pain. We read or hear of children and teens who are bullied in school, on the playground, or in their neighborhood. There are stories of children who are picked on because they are smart—the nerds and geeks—but whose social skills are lacking. There are stories of children who are beaten up or picked on because they do not have the "right" clothes or gym shoes. Some children and teens experience their clothes being stolen because someone else wants them or wants to humiliate the person. The intensity of bullying forces some children and teens to change schools or withdraw into a cocoon state of living.

There are stories of how young people who are bullied become tired and worn down from the constant barrage of victimization and decide to stand up for themselves. Their frustration and pain can enrage them so much that their desire to protect themselves and stop the bully or bullies results in a very harsh reality. One teen, who had been teased for a while, decided that he was tired of being taunted and found himself in jail because he took a bat and hit the teen who had been teasing him.

Bullying is not a new phenomenon nor is this form of harassment limited to children and teens. What is a bully? It is a blustering, quarrelsome, overbearing person who habitually badgers and intimidates smaller or weaker people.

A DOER OF THE WORD

Bullying is not limited to children and teens. Adults can be bullies on the job, in their families, in the community, and in church. However, we are called by Christ *not* to give up on helping others who are considered the least, the left out, the marginalized, and the disenfranchised. We are called to step out of our comfort zone into our families, jobs, communities, our greater society, the world, and even reach out to the abused stranger. Like Zacchaeus, when we are truly transformed, we want to give more than our best to make right whatever we, too, have done wrong. Or, like the Good Samaritan, we should use what we have to care for someone else, find assistance to pitch in and do what we cannot do, and when what we have already given is still not enough—if we can—we should help yet again. Or we should be like the woman in the Court of the Women in the Temple who gave the two coins (all that she had) in the freewill offering. She gave her best not to make someone who had money richer, but to help others. This woman gave out of her need (Luke 21:1–4). When was the last time that we gave out of our need to someone who was even needier?

It is truly a blessing that God loves imperfect people because this means the Lord loves each and every one of us. This may bring a smile to your face or you may be shouting, "thank You, Jesus," because each of us should realize and know that we are *not* perfect. Fortunately, God's love for us and others is not reflective of how we love ourselves or others. The lack of love and cruelty we show to others is not only present in the lives of adults, but also in some of our children and teens. We should always remember that we live and walk in the excellence of Jesus when we show others the love of Christ in us. Can others see the Jesus in you?

PRAYER

Dear God, help others always be able to see the Jesus in us. We desire with all our being to live and walk in Your excellence. Amen.

A KNEE-BENT HEALING

BASED ON MARK 5:25–34

KEY VERSE: *"For [the sick woman] thought to herself, 'If I can just touch his robe, I will be healed'"* (Mark 5:28, NLT).

UP FRONT AND PERSONAL
Mr. and Mrs. G's Story

Life began as it usually did with a cup of black coffee and some toast, and reading the morning paper. Mr. and Mrs. G were usually up before the sun. They had been married for more than 35 years, and they truly loved each other. Their love for each other and their children was deep, and weathered many spectacular and life-giving events. Even when they ran into a bump in the road, their love and commitment to one another was strong. Therefore, today was no different, other than his usual problems of frequent trips to the bathroom. Mr. G was up early and ready to start his day, but something was not quite right.

He was into his usual routine, but he had a strange feeling that something was different. Mr. G kept the thought to himself, but wondered if the meal from the restaurant had bothered him or if something else was wrong. He wondered, but did nothing about it until months later, when the doctor told him that he had prostate cancer.

James and Marie's Story

Thousands of miles away, there was a young couple who had been married for almost two years. Life was both challenging and exciting. The newlyweds worked hard and had a bright future ahead of them. The husband, James, and his wife, Marie, both believed in eating healthy and exercising. James played basketball and ran at least 15 miles a day. He sometimes would enter marathons and always finished somewhere in the middle of the pack. Marie played golf, racquetball, and tennis. Every now and then they both complained of sore muscles and other aches and pains, but by the time each received a loving massage from the other, the pains would seem to dissipate.

James and Marie were in great shape, so when James developed a cough that would not go away, he did not think too much about it. The cough was irritating at times, but after some cough medicine and hot tea, the cough would subside. James thought that the cold he had a few weeks ago was the source of his cough. As time went on, the cold had vanished, but the cough remained.

Finally, after much insistence from Marie, James decided to visit the doctor. The doctor examined James and asked him some questions about his health and about the cough. Because James was in excellent health, he did not have much to say about the cough. After James and the doctor finished their conversation, the doctor told James that he wanted him to have a chest X-ray just to make sure his lungs were clear. James agreed, and had the X-ray the following week.

Taking the X-ray went fine. Neither James nor Marie thought too much about it. James went for his usual early morning run, and even stopped at the local coffee shop to talk to a couple of his fellow runners. After about 15 minutes, James walked the few blocks to his home. As he turned the key in the door, the phone rang. When James picked up the phone, a strange feeling came over him. The doctor was on the other end and asked James if he could come into the office the following day. James quietly asked, "Why?" The doctor told him that he would talk with him "tomorrow at 10:00 a.m." James hung up the phone without saying anything to the doctor and sunk into the thick leather chair in the living room.

When Marie came home, James told her that he had to go to the doctor in the morning, and asked if she would go with him. Marie agreed and they both sat silently and then hugged each other for a long moment. As the sun beckoned the darkness to leave the sky, James played over and over in his mind what the doctor might say. Soon the wait was over. The doctor informed James and Marie that James had lung cancer. James knew that life would be different from this day forward. . .and so did Marie.

Ruth's Story

Forty-year-old Ruth had no intentions of getting a mammogram (breast exam) in the present or near future. After all, she was feeling fine in that area. There were no tell-tale signs of any abnormalities (spots, fluid leaks, discoloration, lumps, or tumors). So when Willa, her sister-in-law, who was also a registered nurse, called early one morning to urge Ruth to have a mammogram taken, she put the conversation quickly on the back burner of her mind. She figured that she would get around to it eventually. After all, she hated going to the doctor. Right then, she was too busy caring for a husband and three children—one in college, one in high school, and the other in junior high—and being a full-time writer.

The next time Ruth talked to Willa, she again urged her to get this much-needed test. Ruth finally agreed under protest. She knew Willa would not rest until she followed through and she knew Willa would keep badgering her. In fact, in that last call that Willa made to Ruth, Willa had dire urgency in her voice.

Finally a few weeks after registering at a local hospital, Ruth did go for the exam. She still had no indications that her life was in danger. Basically, Ruth felt fine. Therefore, when the doctor gave her a clean bill of health and sent her home, she was more than pleased. However, her elation was short-lived. A few hours after arriving home, Ruth received a call to come back to the hospital. It seemed that the staff needed to check her X-ray again. There was a shadow on the X-ray that caused them to be concerned. Ruth rushed back to the hospital, still not appreciating the gravity of the situation. This would just be a routine matter, she thought.

Later, however, she was told that a small mass was showing up on the prints—so small that breast self-examinations could not detect it. It was .03 centimeters. The doctor could not even feel it, but the mammogram detected it. This mass was "suspicious." A few days later, the doctor called and informed Ruth that she had breast cancer.

Chills ran up and down Ruth's spine. She did not even know anyone who had cancer, and definitely did not appreciate what she was in for. Her sister-in-law, Willa, however, had treated many cancer patients, and knew first-hand the gravity of the situation. To help Ruth appreciate her dilemma, Willa gave her several books on the subject. As Ruth read them and internalized the illustrations shown, fear set in. She learned that cancer could be so vicious that it could break off and spread quickly throughout the body. A small tumor could double in size in just a few months. Cancer could even cause death! Therefore, it was imperative that Ruth get into a treatment program immediately!

Subsequently, Ruth's biopsy and tests showed that the cancer had been contained in that one breast, but it was infiltrating. After the lumpectomy (removal of the cancerous lump), her oncologist advised that Ruth undergo both radiation treatments and chemotherapy. She was to report to the hospital ASAP so that she could have a plastered mold made for her so that she could lie in it when taking the radiation treatments. When the rays of the radiation hit her, their aim must always hit the right spot. The mold would assure this.

The next six months taught Ruth how to value life and to appreciate health, strength, family, friends, and smelling the roses. It taught her what was important in life and that acquiring 'things' should be at the bottom of her list. In fact, when she went into the hospital for her biopsy, she had to make a "living will." Ruth learned that even in going through the surgery that she was not guaranteed she would recover from the anesthesia. The doctors did not even know if the cancer was all over her body. Her life was truly in God's hands.

A WORD FROM THE LORD
SCRIPTURE: Mark 5:25–34
PLACE: Capernaum
CHARACTERS: Jesus, the sick woman, the disciples

Mark 5:25, NLT A woman in the crowd had suffered for twelve years with constant bleeding. **26** She had suffered a great deal from many doctors, and over the years she had spent everything she had to pay them, but she had gotten no better. In fact, she had gotten worse. **27** She had heard about Jesus, so she came up behind him through the crowd and touched his robe. **28** For she thought to herself, "If I can just touch his robe, I will be healed." **29** Immediately the bleeding stopped, and she could feel in her body that she had been healed of her terrible condition. **30** Jesus realized at once that healing power had gone out from him, so he turned around in the crowd and asked, "Who touched my robe?" **31** His disciples said to him, "Look at this crowd pressing around you. How can you ask, 'Who touched me?'" **32** But he kept on looking around to see who had done it. **33** Then the frightened woman, trembling at the realization of what had happened to her, came and fell to her knees in front of him and told him what she had done. **34** And he said to her, "Daughter, your faith has made you well. Go in peace. Your suffering is over."

BACKGROUND

NAME: Unknown (called "a certain woman" in the Kings James Version of the Bible)
FAMILY ORIGIN: Unknown
AGE: Unknown
MARITAL STATUS: Unknown
OCCUPATION: Unknown
CHILDREN: Unknown
RESIDENCE: probably at Capernaum

The gospel of Mark is filled with many miracle-healing stories of Jesus. In chapters 1–3:12, before Jesus called all 12 of His disciples, He healed many of various illnesses, even some through what we call exorcisms (driving out evil spirits) today. He also restored the man who came begging on his knees for Jesus to heal him from leprosy. Mark gives us powerful stories of Jesus' healing powers, his attention, and compassion. One of the highlighted stories in Mark 5:25–34 is the woman with the blood disease.

Mark sets the stage for this medical miracle, "And a large crowd followed him and pressed in on him" (Mark 5:24). As you read the story, note that Mark's use of the adjective "large" in describing the size of the crowd is both important and significant. Earlier in the chapter, he has shared with us the healing of the possessed man or how Jesus freed this man from demoniac spirits. Now, we learn of Jesus' healing power with the walking-wounded woman and a dead child. As is often the case, in Jesus' healing ministry, He walks among the people and someone receives a life-changing experience. This time, Mark shows us, through his fast-paced storytelling, that the woman with an incurable blood disease will be blessed in a mighty way.

Let us journey with Mark (5:25) as we share in this healing story that includes an "unnamed" woman, a large group of people, the disciples, and Jesus. For 12 long years—4,340 days—she lived with bleeding every day of her life. Because of the disease and the many physicians she had visited, her hemorrhaging left her with depleted funds. Not only was this unnamed woman broke and living in poverty, but the doctors could not give her any medication to cure her illness. Needless to say, her health declined—"grew worse" (v. 26, RSV). In fact her sickness and having no medical relief in sight were not the end of her terrible plight; in addition, she was left to live as an "untouchable" woman. Because of the blood she lost, she was considered "unclean." It had been established in Leviticus 15:19–31 that a woman was thought to be unclean when she bled. This meant that until she finished her time of purification, she had to live separated from her family and friends. The disease that this woman struggled with daily had left her in a permanent separated status of life (no friends and no family to spend time with laughing, eating a meal together, or just talking about the latest happenings in town).

The nameless woman made a predetermined decision to have a healing encounter with Jesus (Mark 5:27). Mark does not tell us how and when she knew about Jesus' healing power, but he does let us know that she made her way through the crowd. The large crowd served as an initial barrier to her reaching Jesus, as others kept getting in the way. If you have ever been to a crowded church worship service, or a chicken or catfish dinner at church, then you know what she must have felt like being surrounded by all those people. Her destination was Jesus and the crowd was not going to stop her from receiving her healing. Even though Mark does not tell us how and when she knew Jesus, this story reveals to us that she knew He had power.

Having so many people around Jesus probably caused her to press and push to reach Him. As she worked her way through the crowd to Jesus, Mark shares with us a brief mental resignation that she must have thought or even spoke out loud.

Mark writes that she declared, "If I can just touch his clothes, I will be healed" (5:28). The healing power resided in the hem of Jesus' cloak or robe. There was a belief among the Jews that healing power was in the hem of the rabbi's garment. Therefore, the woman knew that if she could just touch the hem of his garment that she would be made whole and restored to health.

This nameless woman either had to bend down to touch the hem of Jesus' cloak, or maybe she was already crawling through the crowd and gently reached up and touched the hem of his garment. However it happened, she bent to touch his garment, and received an immediate response from Jesus. The response was so quick and so amazing that she knew instantly the bleeding stopped, and she was healed from her diseases (Mark 5:29).

Her health was restored, but Jesus did not allow her to walk away or run from this miracle that had just happened. Jesus turned around as soon as the touch and the healing took place and asked a very challenging question, "Who touched my robe?" (Mark 5:30). He did not ask, "Who touched me?" The disciples asked how He could ask, "Who touched me?" (v. 31). He not only responded to the touch, but he wanted to know who touched His garment.

The disciples were amazed that with the large crowd, Jesus would ask a question like that. Jesus waited for the person to come forward. As she obeyed, she trembled in fear and bowed down before Him to share her story (Mark 5:33). After she had finished speaking, Jesus gave her an endearing name and title with a blessing. Jesus first called her, "Daughter," then He gave her the reassurance that she had been healed and that she did not have to worry anymore (v. 34).

What a joy for her to hear that great news and to be called a daughter! Calling her "daughter" reminded her that she was someone dear and worth caring for. Because of the restoration that Jesus had given her, her life would no longer be lived separately. Instead, it would be lived in community with others. Jesus acknowledged that her healing was the result of both her faith and her willingness to step out (act) in faith.

SOMETHING TO THINK ABOUT . . .

Health issues are major problems that must continually be addressed in this country and around the world. In the African American community, we have a long medical list of diseases, health related problems, and issues that require more research opportunities, financial backing, and input from African Americans and the medical communities. In fact the leading causes of death among African Americans in 2003 were: "(1) heart disease; (2) cancer; (3) cerebrovascular disease (stroke); (4) diabetes; (5) accidents; (6) homicide; (7) nephritis, nephritic syndrome, and nephrosis; (8) chronic lower respiratory disease; (9) HIV (AIDS); and (10) septicemia" (Heron and Smith 2006, Table 3).

If we do not consistently and more openly talk and do more to prevent these diseases and the stranglehold of poverty that is associated with them, we are left to die at higher numbers. We are also left trying to heal ourselves without the proper tools to assist us.

One disease that has left an indelible mark in the United States and is increasing in large numbers within the African American community is cancer. At one time, whispering the "C word" was an acceptable social thing to do. Even today, there are individuals who would rather not say they have cancer. We respect their right to keep their medical history to themselves, but it is important that we have access to knowledge so that we can intelligently fight the disease.

Although it is not considered a "secret disease" anymore, some women and men still do not want anyone to know that they had or have cancer. Cancer invades the bodies of persons from various social and racial communities. In 2001, the Intercultural Cancer Council's (ICC) research on cancer in the United States found that "out of 35 million African Americans (we make up 12–13% of the population), 55% of African Americans battling cancer lived mainly in the South, 19% in the Northeast, 18% percent in the Midwest, and 8% in the West" (Iammarino 2001, 1). The usual 12% or 13% of the population was not a new number. It should be noted that "the African American community is equally as diverse as other ethnic and racial populations, and includes people from Nigeria, Ethiopia, South Africa, the West Indies, and other parts of the Caribbean" (2001, 5).

The National Cancer Institute's research on African Americans with cancer (2005, 2) supports the statistics provided by the ICC that "approximately 34.7% of the cancer population in the United States, even though we are about 12–13% of the population" (Iammarino 2005, 1). Both studies indicate that African Americans have disproportionate numbers of various forms of cancer.

According to the NCI study, although "overall age-adjusted cancer incidence rates for African American women are lower than those for Whites, African American women have the highest rates of various forms of cancer than other populations. However, African Americans have the highest incidence rates for certain forms of cancer—colon and rectum and lung and bronchus" (2005, 2).

In the 1990s, cancer among African American women decreased, but there is still a higher percentage of a lower survival rate than Whites for colorectal, lung, breast, and cervical cancers (Cancer Health Disparities 2005, 1–2). Additionally, the statistical data supports the facts that, unlike other communities, cancer is not always focused on or addressed among and for African Americans. For women, it was noted that "disparities in cancer outcomes for African American women are explained in part by not only later stages at diagnosis, but also from less aggressive treatment" (2005, 1). The death rate for African American women is higher for the cancer forms listed above than among other racial/ethnic groups (2005, 2).

The outlook for cancer among African American men is not any better. There are high incidences of prostate, colon and rectum, and lung and bronchus cancer among this group (Cancer Health Disparities 2005, 3). While women may respond quicker once the diagnosis or information is provided, men do not respond to taking care of medical needs with the same vigor. Addressing medical issues in earlier stages would give men a greater chance of survival. However, African American men die of prostate cancer at a rate of 68.1% compared to 27.7% for Whites, 18.3% to American Indians/Alaska Natives, Hispanics/Latinos 38.7% and Asians/Pacific Islanders 39.4% (2005, 3).

A startling study for some may be that in 1999, the ICC research showed that the cancer among African American children, ages 1–14 years, ranks third among the leading causes of death. It is surpassed only by accidents and homicides (Iammarino 2005, 1).

A DOER OF THE WORD

In this light, we must work to stop the violence and other problems that are plaguing our community. In addition, we need to address the medical concerns that beset us in many ways. Taken as a whole, then, we need strong and healthy children equipped with sharp minds to help meet our present and future challenges.

There are several ways that we can assist in creating and advocating a better healthy system and community for ourselves and others. Diet is extremely important. Study after study shows that it is important to eat foods that are healthy and nutritionally beneficial. The major factors that contribute to the high rate of cancer among African Americans are tied to the "quality of health" and the socioeconomic conditions (Cancer Answers 2005, 1, 2). There is a need for African Americans to assist, whenever and wherever possible, in reducing the risks of cancer. This can be done by cultivating a steady "exercise program, maintaining a healthy diet, and, most of all, not smoking" (2005, 1).

The socioeconomic components cannot be ignored—from diet to health insurance—when investigating the risks related to cancer. African Americans who are poor do not have access to better food choices. Also the lack of insurance contributes to persons not seeking medical attention earlier and the opportunity to have services available for their medical needs.

Research notes that African Americans "who have high levels of education, income, and good health insurance have cancer death rates that are closer to the general population, and lower cancer death rates than impoverished African Americans" (Cancer Answers 2005, 2). At the same time, research states that preliminary cancer data shows that African American men, "regardless of income, and level of and access to health insurance," have far higher rates of developing prostate cancer than White men (2005, 2).

Cancer is a serious disease that requires us to investigate vigorously and to practice preventive care as much as possible. When we do nothing to bolster the quality of health care in the African American community, life is at stake and the quality of our lives are the high premiums we pay. Therefore, we should avoid bad eating habits, lobby for a better health care system, work to change the systems that create poverty, and help to meet the basic needs of the poor. Cancer is not disappearing from our lives today, but we can hope that we are a part of the solutions for its eradication tomorrow.

PRAYER

Dear Lord, thank You for giving us the opportunity to lighten the burden of those who are sick. Thank You also for Your healing powers and the ability You have given us as healing and change agents in this world. To make a difference in how we treat one another, show us how to challenge people and their systems. Amen.

AN EXPENSIVE MEAL

BASED ON DANIEL 1:5–12

KEY VERSE: *"But Daniel was determined not to defile himself by eating the food and wine given to them by the king. He asked the chief of staff for permission not to eat these unacceptable foods"* (Daniel 1:8, NLT).

UP FRONT AND PERSONAL

He tried to sleep, but rest eluded him. His wife slept, but she tossed and turned all night long. "What would they do?" Because they generated new ideas to bring their kinfolk together, they were affectionately called the "Genesis" family by their own relatives and neighbors. Their innovations became a tradition.

The wife loved her handsome husband, but he snored so loud that a bear would run for cover, and the next door neighbor's dog would howl in the summer when the bedroom window was left open. He also loved his wife, but he wished she would not toss and turn so much. His snoring could not be that bad. Or was it?

Now the lady of the house was charming, pretty, and gave great hugs to the little children at Sunday School, so she thought. But as the children grew older and bigger, they preferred that she not hug them so much because they were more conscious of her size and afraid of her at times. Her pleasing personality had not changed, but they had.

The man of the house was a hard worker and had the best 4th of July celebrations that anyone could imagine. This was a tradition the Genesis couple loved. They never had children of their own, but had been foster parents for more than 20 children.

Don't worry, it was not his snoring that kept them from having children, but the doctor had advised them against having a child because of a rare disease they both had. The child could inherit the disease from both of them. Mr. and Mrs. Genesis had hoped on three different occasions that their baby would be born and be healthy. However, each time ended in a miscarriage. The doctor told them if Mrs. Genesis became pregnant again, she and the baby could both die. Eventually, they decided it was best for them to be parents to children whose biological parents were unable to love and raise them. So now, they had their grandchildren coming home to share in this fun event. This special day was about family, friends (old and new), and good food. They would take time to remember those who had already gone on to their heavenly home and the legacy he or she had left behind.

The fireworks were spectacular and Mr. Genesis could grill a steak that melted in your mouth, make a peach cobbler that even your grandma would fight you over, and could make potatoes say "thank you" for mixing them so well in the potato salad. These were just a few of the scrumptious samples from all the bountiful food that flowed for the 4th of July celebration. Everyone came, so it seemed, and went away a few pounds heavier.

But Mr. Genesis could not rest at night because he loved his food more than he loved or cared to exercise. The food became a way for him to eat and escape from life. Not that he had any more problems than anyone else, but he enjoyed food and food enjoyed him, or so he thought.

Food was his friend and his enemy. In other words, he was guilty of too many expensive meals—meals that could cause him mental, physical, and spiritual problems. The question begs to be asked, "How could he make different choices and change his lifestyle?" He could see a nutritionist or have someone coach him with diet and exercise, but what about his personal choices? Mr. and Mrs. Genesis are loving people, but how can their love become a love that focuses on their own health needs? And how can the church be supportive of your suggestions?

A WORD FROM THE LORD
SCRIPTURE: Daniel 1:5–12
PLACE: Babylon
CHARACTERS: Daniel, Hananiah, Mishael, Azariah
Daniel 1:5, NLT The king assigned them a daily ration of food and wine from his own kitchens. They were to be trained for a three years, and then they would enter the royal service. **6** Daniel, Hananiah, Mishael, and Azariah were four of the young men chosen, all from the tribe of Judah. **7** The chief of staff renamed them with these Babylonian names: Daniel was called Belteshazzar. Hananiah was called Shadrach. Mishael was

called Meshach. Azariah was called Abednego. **8** But Daniel was determined not to defile himself by eating the food and wine given to them by the king. He asked the chief of staff for permission not to eat these unacceptable foods. **9** Now God had given the chief of staff both respect and affection for Daniel. **10** But he responded, "I am afraid of my lord the king, who has ordered that you eat this food and wine. If you become pale and thin compared to the other youths your age, I am afraid the king will have me beheaded." **11** Daniel spoke with the attendant who had been appointed by the chief of staff to look after Daniel, Hananiah, Mishael, and Azariah. **12** "Please test us for ten days on a diet of vegetables and water," Daniel said.

BACKGROUND

NAME: Daniel; his name means "God is my judge" (Barker, et. al. 1995, 1291).
FAMILY ORIGIN: Unknown
AGE: was a youth when he went to Babylon into captivity and many Israelites were there 70 years
MARITAL STATUS: Unknown
OCCUPATION: a captive from Israel who became an adviser to two Babylonian kings (Nebuchadnezzar, Belshazzar) and two Medo-Persian kings (Darius, Cyrus)
CHILDREN: Unknown
RESIDENCE: Judah and Babylon

NAME: Hananiah; his name means "the LORD shows grace" (Barker, et. al. 1995, 1291).
FAMILY ORIGIN: Unknown
AGE: was a youth when he went to Babylon into captivity and many Israelites were there 70 years
MARITAL STATUS: Unknown
OCCUPATION: one of the captives appointed by King Nebuchadnezzar's chief official to be an attendant to look after Daniel
CHILDREN: Unknown
RESIDENCE: Judah and Babylon

NAME: Mishael and his name means "who is like God?" (Barker, et. al.

1995, 1263).
FAMILY ORIGIN: Unknown
AGE: was a youth when he went to Babylon into captivity and many Israelites were there 70 years
MARITAL STATUS: Unknown
OCCUPATION: one of the captives appointed by King Nebuchadnezzar's chief official to be an attendant to look after Daniel
CHILDREN: Unknown
RESIDENCE: Judah and Babylon

NAME: Azariah and his name means "the LORD helps" (Barker, et. al. 1995, 1291).
FAMILY ORIGIN: Unknown
AGE: was a youth when he went to Babylon into captivity and many Israelites were there 70 years
MARITAL STATUS: Unknown
OCCUPATION: one of the captives appointed by King Nebuchadnezzar's chief official to be an attendant to look after Daniel
CHILDREN: Unknown
RESIDENCE: Judah and Babylon

The story of Daniel, Hananiah, Mishael, and Azariah is one of the more remarkable sagas of courage, faith, and discipline in the Bible. We know them as Beltzeshazzar, Shadrach, Meshach, and Abednego. To read the full story of what happened to the four young men and how God worked in their lives in miraculous ways, read the entire book of Daniel. Our focus in the book of Daniel is on how Daniel was able to practice courage and discipline although he and many others were living in exile under the ruling power of Babylon's King Nebuchadnezzar.

King Jehoiakim of Judah ruled Jerusalem when Daniel and the three young men were taken into exile, but the Lord had allowed King Nebuchadnezzar to take Jerusalem (Daniel 1:2). Daniel and his country-men could have given up and followed the ways of the king, but they did not give up on God. Forced to live in a new country and accept new religious, social, and cultural values, Daniel and all who were kidnapped and taken to live in Babylon had to adjust to a different way of living, which challenged their faith.

In the story of Daniel, we see how faith in the Lord was a blessing. Our main character chose a way of life that was pleasing to Almighty God, regardless of pain, suffering, and even death.

Verse 5 begins with an introduction of the "expensive" meal the king had declared that the men, who were considered the best servants for the palace and the king, were to be served daily. It included only "royal food and wine." They were also to be educated for three years. This was an expensive meal for the new subjects of the king—expensive not only in the cost, but in the price they would have to pay for eating and drinking from the king's table. The food was the finest and the wine would come from the best fruit in the land.

Those who were chosen to study and eat the king's food had to be a quick study and learn the language and literature of Babylon, classical literature in Sumerian and Akadian cuneiform (Barker, et. al. 1995, 1291), science, history, mathematics, astronomy, and magic (Life Application Study Bible 1996, 1594). In this Chaldean culture, they would have to learn how to speak Aramaic and the very complicated language of Babylon (1996, 1594). In addition, the young men who were chosen had to quickly learn new ideas and concepts, physically look the part, and appear to be disciplined with aptitude and attitude.

It was not long before the palace master, the "chief eunuch," changed their names to Beltseshazzar, Shadrach, Meshach, and Abednego (Daniel 1:7). We do not know the name of the chief eunuch, but we do know that he was very important to Daniel and the other young men's survival in the palace. Although the palace master changed their names, the book of Daniel does not use Daniel's new name, and the new names of the other young men are not used until later in chapter 2.

The Lord allowed Daniel to have "favor," in other words, to be liked by the palace master and work out a deal with him regarding his new diet (Daniel 1:8–11). The palace master was concerned that Daniel would not eat the food or drink the wine that the king had commanded, so he shared his concern, and Daniel gave him another way to handle the situation. He listened to Daniel's plan, which consisted of only feeding some of the young men vegetables and water for 10 days and to compare how they looked with those who would eat the king's food and drink his wine (v. 12). After the end of the allotted 10 days, the palace master would see if the plan worked.

In fact, Daniel, Hananiah, Mishael, and Azariah looked quite healthy after the 10 days. The palace master, then, decided that the young men could continue eating food that would not defile their body and their healthy look would save all their lives, including the palace master's (Daniel 1:12–16).

SOMETHING TO THINK ABOUT . . .

The fact that countries invade other countries and people are forced to live in ways that create major changes in their lives is not new. Since 2003, we have been in a war in Iraq. As a result, many American lives have been changed or lost.

The United States has had its own Revolutionary War, Civil War, World Wars I and II, in addition to the Korean Conflict (war to many), and the Vietnam War. Hence, war is not unfamiliar to our country. Of course there is death, destruction, families are torn apart, and religious beliefs are reframed or denied. All are a part of what happens when war takes place within a country or countries participating in the war. Consequently, having a strong individual and collective faith base will provide a sense of hope and determination to help individuals hold on while undergoing the vast transformations that are happening and will happen. Our Scripture story reminds us of how land invasions and war will cause people to accept a new way of living and how being grounded in their faith will provide individuals with an inner strength to make it.

African American history has similarities to the story of Daniel, Shadrach, Meshach, and Abednego in that their names were changed to break the bond with their identity, cultural values, and religious beliefs. Changing someone's name forces them, at some point, to refocus who they are in relationship to where they are and who is in control. Changing someone's name encourages us not to remember where we come from and who we are. A new name will have a different sound and a different meaning. King Darius was determined to have his new subjects worship him and bow down to his way of living. African Americans have a history of our ancestors' names being changed when they were brought to this country as slaves and as their children were being born here. In the famous movie and book *Roots* by Alex Haley, we are reminded how one strong African man named "Kunta Kinte" refused to be called "Toby." Yet, through much violence and physical and emotional stress, he was forced to accept his new name.

As a people, we continue to use very traditional English names such as "John" and "Michael," but some of us are very colorful and will break out of certain strongholds as time goes on—and names are one of them. African names among African American born children are not new, so we will here names like Sekou, which means "fighter" or Amani, which means "faith." We also sometimes hear variations on names that 99% identifies our race. We would be surprised if "Shaniquah" (spelled many ways) or "Shanene" were not Black women. For African American males, "Leroy" had been a dominant name. However in recent years, DaShawn, or Jamaal (Jamal), etc. has dominated the culture. Studies reported on national television and radio reveal that, unfortunately, having a name that identifies one as Black or African American (especially male) can subject one to discrimination when applying for a job, housing, etc. Although we cannot force people to like our names and our cultural choices, claiming our identity through the names we choose should be decision that is not disrespected or abused by others. The creativity in naming someone is unique, personal, and in the context of the community.

A DOER OF THE WORD

Daniel was disciplined and he trusted God. Fine food was not his choice or the desire of his friends. Eating vegetables and drinking water instead of the king's wine and royal food proved to be a healthy and was a faith decision for them.

Making healthy food and drinking selections and trusting in God to care for us would give so many African Americans healthier lives. Many of our health problems are tied to our diets. We are what we eat, don't eat, and what we don't exercise off or shape up. It is not hard to look at the myriad of health issues that affect us as a people and see that food and drink are connected. Diabetes, obesity, high blood pressure/hypertension, heart disease, and cholesterol are some of the various medical concerns that affect African Americans at an alarming rate. When we have poor health or drug-managed health issues, we are impacted financially, physically, psychologically, socially, and spiritually.

Good to great health is a blessing and is something that we can learn to create in our own lives. Taking responsibility for what we can control and doing something about major health concerns are vital steps to living life in the abundance of being a new creature in Christ Jesus. We must remember that some meals are too expensive for us mentally, physically, and spiritually! Some meals do not lead to excellence in our walk with our God.

PRAYER

Dear God, thank You for the body (temple) that You have given us. Please help us to remember that some meals are too expensive for us to eat. Also help us to worship You by taking good care of our temples that are on loan from You. Amen.

TROUBLE IN THE CAMP

BASED ON JOSHUA 6:16–21; 7:1, 10–13, 20–21

KEY VERSE: *"But Israel violated the instructions about the things set apart for the LORD. A man named Achan had stolen some of these dedicated things, so the LORD was very angry with the Israelites. Achan was the son of Carmi, a descendant of Zimri son of Zerah, of the tribe of Judah"* (Joshua 7:1, NLT).

UP FRONT AND PERSONAL

In school, Marcus always seemed nice, but slightly troubled. Claude D, his brother, was also quite strong and smart, but was the rough and tough type that you would think twice about starting any trouble with. The nice one, whom everyone loved, was named Marcus, and his brother, whom everyone respected, was named Claude D. Because he thought it added a sense of pride and character to his name, Claude D added the letter D to his name. He did this when he was about 8 years old and no one made him change it. The adults thought it was cute and manly for him to do this, so they left him alone.

Marcus had a charming personality and was smart, but there was still something about him. No one was sure what it was, but they knew he was just *slightly different*. Marcus was the type of boy that everyone wanted to be around, and they felt good about themselves when they left his presence. Yet, as time went on, they knew that they couldn't put their finger on it, but something was slightly askew about him.

Well, time has a way of proving you right or wrong. Claude D and Marcus came from a "good" family. Their parents were active members of the church, who lived out what they learned and taught in church. Their mother was the first woman deacon at the church. This upset many people at first, but she prayed and proved to them that she could handle "man's work." Their father was the handyman of the church and really loved the Lord. He attended prayer meetings regularly, taught Sunday School to young men, and until the square box stores slowly crept in, he had the best corner store in town. He saw what was happening early on, but until they saw what he saw and experienced what he experienced, everyone complained when he closed the store.

The brothers grew up and went into businesses for themselves. Claude D owned a variety of health food stores and spas in various locations in the region. Marcus owned a real estate business. One day, out of the blue, Marcus disappeared. His family—a wonderful wife, three great kids, and a loving dog—had no idea what happened to him. They were so sad and heartbroken that they prayed and prayed, but Marcus did not return. His brother, Claude D, with his warm and fun-loving family, prayed and prayed as well. Their church families in the town of Smithville also prayed and prayed.

In fact, Claude D belonged to the best Baptist church in town and Marcus belonged to the best AME church in town. Both churches had annual "Watch Night" services with the other denominations—CME, Pentecostal, Apostolic, Church of God, Church of God in Christ, and Presbyterian. Claude D and Marcus' churches would host the services, and the other denominations would decide who would preach and what the Watch Night snacks would be.

In view of Marcus' disappearance, everyone prayed and prayed. They asked themselves, "What happened to Marcus? He was nice and had a wonderful family, but was slightly different."

Because Marcus was not the type to leave home and never call or communicate in some way, many years passed and the family painstakingly declared him dead. They had a memorial service for him and people said the usual nice things about a nice person, but everyone wondered what happened to Marcus.

After his children grew up, married, and had children of their own, the "what happened to Marcus?" rumor mill began to turn again. It proved to be right this time. Marcus was found; but it was a very sad occasion. He was found dead and buried in a makeshift grave outside of town. It seems that a dog, which had been running over the makeshift grave, found a small notebook that he always kept with him. It was on top of the grave. Written in the notebook were these words: "Here lies Marcus Smith. A nice man, but slightly different."

Now it was known what made him different. He was a quiet thief who stole money from wherever he could, whenever he could. In fact, he died as a result of one of his thefts. Marcus had just stolen some money and as he was jumping over a creek, he fell and hit his head on a rock.

He called for help, but no one heard the cry. Marcus repented of his si before he died. The silence honored his request.

A WORD FROM THE LORD

SCRIPTURE: Joshua 6:16–21; 7:1, 10–13, 20–21
PLACE: the Promised Land, Canaan (Jericho)
CHARACTERS: Joshua, Achan, the Priests

Joshua 6:16, NLT The seventh time around, as the priests sounded the long blast on their horns, Joshua commanded the people, "Shout! For the LORD has given you the town! **17** Jericho and everything in it must be completely destroyed as an offering to the LORD. Only Rahab the prostitute and the others in her house will be spared, for she protected our spies. **18** "Do not take any of the things set apart for destruction, or you yourselves will be completely destroyed, and you will bring trouble on the camp of Israel. **19** Everything made from silver, gold, bronze, or iron is sacred to the LORD and must be brought into his treasury." **20** When the people heard the sound of the rams' horns, they shouted as loud as they could. Suddenly, the walls of Jericho collapsed, and the Israelites charged straight into the town and captured it. **21** They completely destroyed everything in it with their swords— men and women, young and old, cattle, sheep, goats, and donkeys.

7:1 But Israel violated the instructions about the things set apart for the LORD. A man named Achan had stolen some of these dedicated things, so the LORD was very angry with the Israelites. Achan was the son of Carmi, a descendant of Zimri son of Zerah, of the tribe of Judah.

7:10 But the LORD said to Joshua, "Get up! Why are you lying on your face like this? **11** Israel has sinned and broken my covenant! They have stolen some of the things that I commanded must be set apart for me. And they have not only stolen them but have lied about it and hidden the things among their own belongings. **12** That is why the Israelites are running from their enemies in defeat. For now Israel itself has been set apart for destruction. I will not remain with you any longer unless you destroy the things among you that were set apart for destruction. **13** "Get up! Command the people to purify themselves in preparation for tomorrow. For this is what the LORD, the God of Israel, says: Hidden among you, O Israel, are things set apart for the LORD. You will never defeat your enemies until you remove these things from among you.

7:20 Achan replied, "It is true! I have sinned against the LORD, the God of Israel. **21** Among the plunder I saw a beautiful robe from Babylon, 200 silver coins, and a bar of gold weighing more than a pound. I wanted them so much that I took them. They are hidden in the ground beneath my tent, with the silver buried deeper than the rest."

BACKGROUND
NAME: Joshua
FAMILY ORIGIN: the son of Nun
AGE: Unknown
MARITAL STATUS: Married
OCCUPATION: military leader, spy, husband, father, devout follower of God, had been a spokesperson for Moses
CHILDREN: He was a father.
RESIDENCE: Jericho

NAME: Achan
FAMILY ORIGIN: the son of Carmi, of the family of Zimri, of the clan of Zerah, and of the tribe of Judah (Joshua 7:1)
AGE: Unknown
MARITAL STATUS: Married
OCCUPATION: husband, father, spy, thief
CHILDREN: He was a father.
RESIDENCE: entering the Promised Land, Canaan

Now that Moses had gone on to glory with the Lord, Joshua was the leader of the people. After Moses' death, God's chosen people (the Children of Israel—ex-slaves) needed strong leadership, and Joshua was the man. He was a courageous, strong, and righteous leader. Joshua followed the Lord and was able to instill a sense of accomplishment and joy in the people. This was shown in the familiar passage on how Joshua and the people fought the battle of Jericho and the "walls came tumbling down."

In this battle of Jericho, God made it clear to Joshua and all who participated that He was in charge of both the battle and the victory, and He did not need Israel's weapons and expertise. God's military maneuver (they marched around the walls seven times) tested Israel's faith in the God they served to deliver in times of need.

They heard the "victory cry" of the trumpets throughout the city. Under the leadership of Joshua, God's chosen leader of the people, the ex-slaves heralded the sound of victory as the priests blew the trumpets and the walls came tumbling down. Initially, in Joshua 6:10–12, Joshua prepared the Israelites for their victory sound and march. He ordered them not to shout any war sounds, lift their voices, or do anything until he told them to do so with very loud voices. Joshua wanted them to open their mouths and really let go. In addition, Joshua had the seven priests carry the seven trumpets and the ark of the Lord (v. 13), signifying God's presence with them.

The playing of the trumpet was part of a traditional ceremonial celebration that represented tearing down the walls of Jericho. Blowing the trumpet and marching around the walls of Jericho seven times was very significant. As noted by some scholars, the number seven is displayed by having "seven priests, seven trumpets, seven days, seven encirclements on the seventh day, and a seventh-day climactic victory. The preponderance of sevens recalls the seven days of creation (Genesis 1), implying the creation of a new order in the land and continuing the ritual land claim of chapters 3:1–5:12" (Coogan, et. al. 2001, 323).

During this time of seven days of marching and blowing the trumpet, the people were prepared to take the city. They would perform their ritual and then return to their camp (Joshua 6:14). Finally on day seven, they woke up early in the morning and marched around the wall one more time. Then Joshua gave the sign for them to "shout" the victory and they did. Only Rahab and her family would be saved from the utter destruction, and takeover of the city; this was due to the fact that the spies had promised to save her and her family if she was able to help them escape to safety. Joshua made them keep their promise and Rahab and her family were saved (vv. 16–17).

Joshua reminded the ex-slaves not to take those things that had been banned under Moses, which included animals and property (Joshua 6:18). Those things, which could be placed into the "Lord's treasury" (v. 18), were gold, bronze, iron, and silver (v. 19). Joshua also stated that if anyone violated God's orders, it would bring individual destruction as well as destruction to the Israelites as a community (Joshua 6:18). Later, Achan's disobedience showed what happened if someone did not follow God's law, based on what goes into the treasury of the Lord.

After the trumpets sounded and the walls came tumbling down, the men moved with military might into the city. They took the city captive and the Israelites were victorious in the Lord (Joshua 6:20). After they had taken the city and destroyed every living thing in it, the Israelites "dedicated the city to the Lord." Just imagine all the livestock and the people killed! This victory would not leave anyone or anything behind as a reminder of the people or things that were once a part of the city. The Israelites rejoiced in their victory of reaching the land that God had given to them.

In Joshua 7:1, 10–13, 20–21, the sweet smell of victory was in the air, but so was the odor of deceit. Achan was the son of Carmi, a descendant of Zimri son of Zerah, of the tribe of Judah had taken the treasured items for the Lord that was to be given to the Lord. His action made God very angry (v. 1). Achan brought much suffering and pain to the Israelites. Until change in their fate came, the ex-slaves thought they were headed toward the Promised Land and were prepared to win any other battles they needed to win. Achan's stealing the possessions that were to be set aside for the Lord's treasury created a backlash against the men whom Joshua had sent to fight the people of Ai. God, through Joshua, sent three thousand men but they had to run in fear from the Ai soldiers. Because at least 36 of the men were killed, the people lost their courage (vv. 4–6).

Joshua didn't have any idea what Achan had done. The people also did not know why God was not with them. They did know, however, that they had traveled and fought; but the Lord's presence was not with them now. Due to the circumstances, their fear became greater than their faith. Exchanging fear for faith was a story that they lived with throughout their history.

Joshua was so upset with the outcome of the battle that he tore his clothes and cried out to the Lord for help. He pleaded their case and wanted to know why they were all going through this time of failure (Joshua 7:6–9). Joshua fell on the ground and the Lord told him to get up. Then God told him about Israel's sin. The stolen goods were reminders of deceit that had occurred before God (vv. 10–12). God told Joshua to tell the people to "sanctify" (purify) themselves before the Lord. In addition, he told them that if the "dedicated"—stolen goods—were not taken away, the Lord would not be with them before their enemies (v. 13).

The death sentence that the perpetrator must face is found in verse 15. Whoever is found to have committed this crime will be "burned with fire and everything that he has (Joshua 7:15, NLT). Joshua set in motion a plan to have all the tribes and each member, one by one, answer the question they had committed the crime of stealing. It did not take long before Achan admitted that he was the culprit. He even described what he had taken—"a beautiful robe from Babylon, 200 silver coins, and a bar of gold weighing more than a pound" (v. 21, NLT).

The Scripture does not end with Achan sharing what he had taken. The consequences of Achan's actions and the Lord allowing the Israelites to again have victory are crucial to this story. If we do not even mention the consequences of his actions, then we leave out an important part of the story. To fight their enemies and be victorious, Achan's admission allowed the people to have the presence of the Lord with them. Yet the sin of Achan affected his whole family and their survival in a very devastating way. All of them were marched before the people in the camp and Achan was burned first; then the family was stoned to death. The sin of the father definitely affected the family unto their death. Then they were all burned to death and their ashes were left behind. After stoning and burning them all, Joshua and the other Israelites put a large pile of rocks as a monument to what had occurred. The monument is called the "Valley of Trouble" (Joshua 7:24–26, NLT).

Achan violated the law and he caused his family to suffer under what was practiced within the principle of community solidarity. The whole family was represented in one member (especially the head of that community [Barker, et. al. 1995, 298]). He and his family were stoned because he was "found guilty of violating the covenant of the Holy Lord" as found in "Exodus 19:13 and Leviticus 24:23" (1995, 298). They were all burned to cleanse the "land of the evil" that had been there (1995, 298).

SOMETHING TO THINK ABOUT . . .

What individual family members do and how they choose to live their lives are very important to the survival and well-being of the whole family. There are some things that our family members do that we can excuse and some things that we *should not*. We should also remember that *not* thinking or talking about "it" will not make "it" go away. When we do not talk about whatever it is and work toward solving or helping to ease the pain, then we are left with those "closet" secrets that linger and cause irreparable damage to both the perpetrator and to us.

Achan's story is a very dramatic and damaging example of how our actions greatly affect others. Yet, we have family members, including our-selves, who do not share in a community response to their actions. We can

be selfish and want things to go our way. Our way may not be the best wa
to go, and the family suffers.

Once there was a story told about a mother who grew up in a dysfunc
tional home (as almost everyone seems to) that never learned she wa
worth more than her chosen life profession. She had developed a skill lik
Achan's—stealing. She never learned that she could do more than steal fc
a living. In fact, what made the story pronounced or infamous was the fac
that she taught her children the same skill. This mother believed that he
way of living was a valuable tool for her children. So they learned how t
steal and they also ended up in jail as she had.

Subsequently, she was upset because the courts deemed she wa
responsible for her children's lifestyle. Passing on this skill to her childre
only created more problems and trouble for them, and did not give any c
them the freedom that she thought it would.

When we look at our own families and hear about various families on th
news, it is clear that there are families that seem to pass on their bad habit
and/or sin to other members. There are family members who are involve
in drug trafficking—including bringing the drugs into the country (althoug
the majority are not African Americans)—using drugs, exploiting people i
financial and real estate deals, and flaunting their riches or power openl
These are just a few of the sins and the problems that we face, pass on, c
allow our family members to share in willingly or unwillingly.

Although the media and word of mouth help to keep the lies alive tha
as a people, African Americans are most likely to exploit drugs and hu
other people, many of these issues and more are not limited to race or ge
der. If the truth is told, it is true that we have *some* people who are Africa
American that will hurt, humiliate, and hunt down people in multiple wa
for their own good and by any means necessary. They are not concerne
about their family, race, or the group; their own personal satisfaction is the
reward.

How do we keep family members from becoming another statistic ar
another trash pile of pain? Well, one way is to recognize and appreciate th
passing on the pain of domestic violence must be stopped. When movi
came out showing the blatant abuse, there was an outcry by some Africa
American men in the community, in particular, who felt that we were airir
our dirty laundry. Yet women were and are beaten and killed every day l
men who believe they can do this because of what they have inherited fro

their fathers and seen from other men around them. Women stay in these abusive relationships because of fear, how they were raised, and not know-ing how to escape.

The questions beg to be asked, 'When and how do we stop the vicious cycle of domestic abuse? When does the church step in and provide assis-tance or preventive care?'

A DOER OF THE WORD

So that we can be catalysts for change, these major issues should always be present before us. However, we also need to address how we can pass on the values of having good common sense, money management, a mis-sionary or caring mentality, and making a difference for justice in an unjust world. We know that we cannot force changes of the heart, but we can pur-pose in our hearts to treat each other better—with more love, care, and respect. We can also become advocates for better laws in regulating hous-ing and eradicating poverty. We also need to challenge financial institutions who charge enormous prices for consumer goods and credit cards. In addi-tion, we can teach our children how to build generational wealth, a better work ethic, and develop common sense solutions to our many problems. How can we do this and where would we start?

Common sense-building, in everyday life experiences, starts by studying, internalizing, and walking in God's Word. Therefore, we should do as Jesus said to do, "'Love the Lord your God with all your heart and with all your soul and with all your strength and with all your mind'; and, 'Love your neighbor as yourself'" (Luke 10:27, NIV). If we are not willing to love our-selves in positive and healthy ways, then we cannot truly love others. If we are not willing to love God with everything that is within us, then we will choose to do things that are destructive and hurtful to others.

Also, not doing so much for our children and allowing them to give back to God and their communities at an early age will help them have a more compassionate heart. Learning about other customs, languages, traditions, and the actual land provides a better understanding of how other people live. Purposefully helping others who struggle in life is very necessary to break down the barriers between the haves and the have nots. Poverty is very real and money does talk and makes things happen in this world. Praying and being wise as serpents and gentle as doves do change things. However, as we pass on good things to our children, family, friends, and the world, we must "watch and pray" (Matthew 26:41, NIV). What is the visible and the invisible legacy that you hope you will leave behind?

PRAYER

LORD, *help us to pass on the baton of life: joy, happiness, truth, faith, and a spirit to work through the difficult times. We want to be worthy of walking with You, so allow us to accept Jesus in our hearts. Then because Your light overshadows the darkness in our families and in our pain, always be our guide and lead us to that light. Finally, bring us together as a community and let us shout the victory of Your peace and power. In the peace and power of Jesus, Amen.*

WORKING HARD OR HARDLY WORKING?

BASED ON NEHEMIAH 1:3–4; 4:1–9; 5:15–16

KEY VERSE: *"At last the wall was completed to half its height around the entire city, for the people had worked with enthusiasm"* (Nehemiah 4:6, NLT).

UP FRONT AND PERSONAL

Life presents us with many challenges that can sometimes break our spirits or push us to overcome the obstacles that are before us. Dr. Percy Julian, a chemist, a Civil Rights activist, a devoted husband and father, and a man of courage, exemplifies the attitude of working through in spite of racism and the pressures of life. This extraordinary man of valor, intellect, compassion, and integrity was born in 1899 in Montgomery, Alabama, He graduated from DePauw University in 1920. His keen academic ability and his love of science were developed further through his studies at Harvard and the University of Vienna. Dr. Julian earned his M.S. from Harvard and his doctorate from the University of Vienna.

His ability to persevere is rooted in his relationship with God, having a supportive and loving family, and his tenacity. Dr. Julian was named Chicago's Man of the Year in 1950, and was "the first Black man and first lay-man to head the Council for Social Action of the Congregational Christian Churches" (Historical Society of Oak Park and River Forest 2003, paragraph 3). Fighting for the rights of others and protecting his family were quite difficult at times. When others are hurling insults, bombs, and setting fire to your home, life and trust in Jesus take on a different meaning.

Dr. Julian was on the faculty of Howard University and the faculty of DePauw University. He was a prolific writer and researcher as well. His studies in both organic and natural chemistry, coupled with his strong interest to help others in scientific and humanitarian ways, propelled him into discoveries to help those who were suffering. When Dr. Julian was on staff at DePauw University and conducting research, he discovered a treatment for glaucoma while working with Dr. Josef Pikl, through a structure called

physostigmine. He became internationally recognized as his discovery wa
published in the *Journal of the American Chemical Society.* Although he was high
ly respected for his work as a scientist, he was not offered the title of prc
fessor since he was Black.

Dr. Julian's work opened a new door of opportunity for him at the Glidde
Company, a paint and varnish company in Chicago. In addition to finding
treatment for glaucoma, his research with the soybean yielded ways to us
the proteins from soybeans to "manufacture such products as paper coat
ings, water-based paints, and textile sizings" (Dr. Percy Julian, paragraph 3

In addition to these contributions and others, Dr. Julian found a way t
isolate "the soya protein, which became the basis for Aero-Foam, the fir
extinguishing material that saw action in World War II" (Historical Societ
of Oak Park and River Forest 2003, paragraph 3).

His humanitarian and scientific greatness not only included the afore
mentioned discoveries, but also more than 130 discoveries to treat glauco
ma and allergies. Dr. Julian is also noted for "his synthesis of cortison
which dramatically reduced the price" and is "highly effective in the trea
ment of rheumatoid arthritis and other inflammatory conditions" (Dr. Perc
Julian, paragraph 5).

During his lifetime, Dr. Julian's legacy of greatness and concern for ot
ers continued in work for social justice for African Americans. Although h
own family's lives were threatened through a bombing and fire set to h
home when they relocated to Oak Park, a suburb of Chicago, he was determine
to pursue his research and to establish a quality life for his family. He gav
speeches and spoke out about the injustices against African Americans.

Despite the racial barriers that were put in his way to stifle his work a
well as harm his family, in 1953 Dr. Julian built a lab in Mexico to further h
research. The lab was met with much resistance, which prevented him fro
opening and operating the lab. When he had no other assistance left, E
Julian received a blessing. Someone came to visit him one day whose life I
had saved a while ago. This grateful man had the means and the ability
help him get the yams he needed for his research. Eventually, through
court battle that he waged with other companies that had been blocke
from doing research work in Mexico, he was able to open his plant.

Dr. Julian was committed to excellence in all aspects of life and was wi
ing to give so much to fulfill his dreams and to help others. His wonderf
contributions are indelibly marked in our lives. In 1993, Dr. Julian's gift

science and humanity was commemorated in a U.S. postal stamp. There are two schools, in Chicago and in Oak Park, that are named after this great man of God (Historical Society of Oak Park and River Forest 2003, paragraph 3).

A WORD FROM THE LORD

SCRIPTURE: Nehemiah 1:3–4; 4:1–9; 5:15–16

PLACE: Jerusalem

CHARACTER: Nehemiah

Nehemiah 1:3, NLT They said to me, "Things are not going well for those who returned to the province of Judah. They are in great trouble and disgrace. The wall of Jerusalem has been torn down, and the gates have been destroyed by fire." **4** When I heard this, I sat down and wept. In fact, for days I mourned, fasted, and prayed to the God of heaven.

4:1 Sanballat was very angry when he learned that we were rebuilding the wall. He flew into a rage and mocked the Jews, **2** saying in front of his friends and the Samarian army officers, "What does this bunch of poor, feeble Jews think they're doing? Do they think they can build the wall in a single day by just offering a few sacrifices? Do they actually think they can make something of stones from a rubbish heap—and charred ones at that?" **3** Tobiah the Ammonite, who was standing beside him, remarked, "That stone wall would collapse if even a fox walked along the top of it!" **4** Then I prayed, "Hear us, our God, for we are being mocked. May their scoffing fall back on their own heads, and may they themselves become captives in a foreign land! **5** Do not ignore their guilt. Do not blot out their sins, for they have provoked you to anger here in front of the builders." **6** At last the wall was completed to half its height around the entire city, for the people had worked with enthusiasm. **7** But when Sanballat and Tobiah and the Arabs, Ammonites, and Ashdodites heard that the work was going ahead and that the gaps in the wall of Jerusalem were being repaired, they were furious. **8** They all made plans to come and fight against Jerusalem and throw us into confusion. **9** But we prayed to our God and guarded the city day and night to protect ourselves.

5:15 The former governors, in contrast, had laid heavy burdens on the people, demanding a daily ration of food and wine, besides forty pieces of silver. Even their assistants took advantage of the people. But because I feared God, I did not act that way. **16** I also devoted myself to working on the wall and refused to acquire any land. And I required all my servants to spend time working on the wall.

BACKGROUND

NAME: Nehemiah; his name means "The Lord Comforts"

FAMILY ORIGIN: son of Hacaliah

AGE: Unknown

MARITAL STATUS: Unknown

OCCUPATION: King's cupbearer, city builder, governor of Judah

CHILDREN: Unknown

RESIDENCE: Persia, Jerusalem

According to Nehemiah 1, on a regular basis the Jewish people had to endure terse and cruel verbal abuse from the various enemy leaders. As you read the first three verses, Sanballat and Tobiah attacked the builders at their core foundation—the internal drive to bring back a way of life that offered hope for the present and future. The leaders' mockery and the taunting of the wall builders, who engaged in the God-given Nehemiah project of rebuilding the wall, loudly proclaimed their fierce determination to weaken the builders' faith and belief. So that these leaders could continue having their position and power, they lashed out with words to hurt and dissuade the workers. They used three fear-evoking approaches to help dismantle the wall: intimidation (4:1–23), economic hardships (5:1–19), and plans to murder Nehemiah (6:1–4; Coogan, et. al. 2001, 692).

Initially, the naysayer, Sanballat, used tactics of intimidation and jeers at what they were doing. He knew once they built the wall that his authority would not be as great. Therefore, he teased the Jews and said, "What are those feeble Jews doing? Will they restore their wall? Will they offer sacrifice? Will they finish in a day? Can they bring the stones back to life out of those heaps of rubble as they are?" (Nehemiah 4:2, paraphrased).

The bullying continued with Tobiah the Ammorite. He made fun of the Jewish workers' skills and their ability to complete a very strenuous job. Verse 3 says that he made fun of their efforts. He said, "That stone wall would collapse if even a fox walked along the top of it!" (Nehemiah 4:3, NLT). "Archeological excavations found Nehemiah's wall to be about nine feet thick" (Breneman 1993, 194; Kenyon 1967, 108). Nine feet thick is a very solid wall, and a fox or any small animal would not have been able to knock it down. Therefore, hard and excellent work makes for a great outcome.

Nehemiah 4:7–8 continues with the opposing leaders plotting and planning to make life very problematic for the Jews. They determined together how they would work in conjunction and cause chaos among the people. The leaders were very angry that the builders would not stop their building, nor would they slow down the work (v. 7). Therefore, the workers continued working and the angry leaders continued getting more upset by the moment. For the most part, the constant picking and verbal pecking at them did not work. In fact, when the verbal abuse began to wear the people down, they completed the wall in 52 days (6:15–16).

Nehemiah's leadership skills, ingenuity, and palace support greatly assisted in the development and the final stone being laid for the wall. Yet, Nehemiah's relationship with God and his strong prayer life were the key components that gave him the foundation and the support he needed to stay focused on his goals, give others hope, and finish the job. In Nehemiah 4:4–5, 9, Nehemiah's prayers were direct and clear. The words of Nehemiah's prayer conveyed that he wanted the enemy exposed and God to take care of them in a mighty way. It has been stated that Nehemiah's prayer was for the enemies of the Jews to receive "divine justice" and not to "spell out the penalties he literally intended" (Breneman 1993, 394–395). In verse 9, his prayer shared his concern and belief that God would take care of the Jewish people.

Nehemiah prayed and watched. He ensured the safety of the people by adding guards to watch out for any surprise attacks. His faith and prayer life reminds us that trusting God, watching, and taking the necessary actions to protect and defend our plans and work are often needed.

SOMETHING TO THINK ABOUT . . .

The story of Nehemiah and the rebuilding of the Jerusalem wall evokes many thoughts and feelings that are akin to the struggles of so many people around the world who are forced to live life at the mercy of stronger militaries and ideologies. In Darfur, over 400,000 people have been murdered because of genocide in the country. Genocide is planned annihilation of a racial, political, or cultural group. There are some individuals, organizations, and churches that have responded to the need to stop this violence. What have you done to address this cruel way of treating other human beings?

We, too, have heard the stories of the cruel journey of the Middle Passage of our ancestors to the United States as well as the journey from Africa to South America. Working hard and fighting obstacles are not strangers to us.

The history and legacy of Africans and African Americans in this country are very deeply woven into the foundation of this country. Giving more than our share, creating, inventing, working hard, caring, and surviving and thriving in very adverse conditions are legacies that we are proud to receive from our ancestors and bring into this present generation. Nehemiah and his workers on the wall know hard work and obstacles in many ways, as do many of our ancestors before us and even many African Americans today. From indentured servants to slavery, the history of Africans and African Americans is filled with stories of how so many were able to do so much. Their hard work laid the foundation for so much growth to spring forth and thrive today. This strong foundation is evidenced in multiple facts of everyday and extraordinary life moments. When we reflect on our past, we cannot help but think of many of our pillars of the community and their demands for justice, through various means, that were grounded in their belief in education, diligence to work hard, aggressive assertiveness, and in their respective religious beliefs.

Because of men and women like Frederick Douglass (the great orator, abolitionist, self-educator, writer), Malcolm X (the self-liberator, Civil Rights activist, writer, intellectual genius), Nannie Helen Burroughs (the educator, entrepreneur, Civil Rights activist, defender of women's rights and African American girls and women, in particular), and Annie Malone (the educator, entrepreneur, hair stylist, chemist for hair products), African Americans have much to be proud of.

Joan Higginbotham follows in the footsteps of the African American men and women pioneers in space: Colonel Guion "Guy" Bluford Jr., the first African American to fly in space in 1983; Ronald McNair, who was tragically killed on his second flight on the space shuttle Challenger in 1986; Charles Bolden Jr., who flew on the Columbia in 1986 and on the Discovery in 1990; and Fredrick Drew Gregory, who had been a veteran astronaut since 1979, commanded the first mission of joint space travel between the Americans and the Russians on his fourth flight into space. Astronaut Joan Higginbotham's journey into space in 2006 was forged by Mae Jemison in 1992, a science specialist on the Japanese and American project aboard the shuttle. Within a year of Dr. Jemison's journey into space, Bernard Harris was a mission specialist in 1993 with fellow astronauts from Germany and America.

The number of African American political leaders from the end of slavery during Reconstruction has grown in numerous ways. The run for the highest political office, the president of the United States and other political offices is not a new endeavor. Senator Barack Obama from Illinois is a contender for the democratic nomination in the U.S. presidential election of 2008. Hillary Rodham Clinton will also be running for the democratic nomination. The first woman to run for president of the United States was Victoria Woodhull in 1872. Her running mate was Frederick Douglass. Since then, many more African Americans and women have run for a nomination in their party or as an official candidate in an independent party. Most notably, though, Shirley Chisholm ran for the democratic nomination in 1972 and Jesse Jackson ran for it in 1984 and 1988. Both have been trailblazers and pioneers in making major inroads to the political wheel. Working hard, learning how to preserve, and depending on God have provided a strong foundation for Chisholm, Jackson, and other leaders such as the late Barbara Jordan and Adam Clayton Powell.

Prayer and tenacity are two of the cornerstones of the African American community that have provided much leadership and the backbreaking work to literally build America. The power of prayer is expressed in the Civil Rights Movement to the many faith expressions within the African American community. Looking at the magnificent architectural government buildings in Washington, DC, the handiwork of many African American men went in to construct and maintain the buildings. African American women were cleaning up after other people's stuff, cleaning the White House, and sewing the dresses for the First Ladies of the White House.

Where does our rich history, in spite of racism and segregation, leave us today? As a people we must never forget that racism is alive and well; but we must love Jesus with everything that is within us and forge ahead to constantly exert our intelligence, to study, and to make a difference. As great as we are as a people, we have much to do to deal with all of the issues that face us today.

A DOER OF THE WORD
Nehemiah was faced with many problems, but those faithful to God were able to keep building the wall. Yes, there were people who criticized in order to destroy and weaken some of the faithful. The opposition mounted, but the Israelites' enemies did not prevail. Our faith, community, and the church—for many of us—continue to be bedrocks in our community, in

spite of our many successes and problems. I am sure that many would disagree, but it is a lie to say that churches are not doing anything to address the many social issues that pervade our community, society, and the world.

Many African American churches and individuals assisted others in bringing money and truckloads of food, books, and clothes to help Hurricane Katrina victims. The more that money shifts from government programs, the more the church is expected to help. Is this right? How can the church help to prevent these problems from occurring? Churches do work in the lives of many, but there is always much to do, and we should do God's work pleasing unto the Lord.

As we move toward the future and live in the present, let us share in the hard work. Let us also pray for power to build a stronger community and learn to live life in the fullness of who we are in God, and not who the world continues to create us to be.

PRAYER

Dear God, thank You for walking with us every step of the way. Bless us to be builders of character, hope, and financial stability. Let us also be caretakers of one another, loving what is good over the dehumanizing toys in our lives. Help us to continue to stand strong against the forces that seek to destroy us inwardly and outwardly. Please continue to love us and grant us the peace and wisdom to choose You, even when your light is hidden from our eyes. Grace, peace, and mercy in Jesus, Amen.

ROI: A RETURN ON INVESTMENT

BASED ON MATTHEW 25:14–26, 28

KEY VERSE: *"The servant to whom he had entrusted the five bags of silver came forward with five more and said, 'Master, you gave me five bags of silver to invest, and I have earned five more.' 'The master was full of praise. "Well done, my good and faithful servant. You have been faithful in handling this small amount, so now I will give you many more responsibilities. Let's celebrate together!"'"* (Matthew 25:20–21, NLT).

UP FRONT AND PERSONAL

Some people have this uncanny belief that we can do so many things all by ourselves and no one has helped us along the way. There are moments, as a friend of mine always says, that people suffer from "convenient amnesia." Convenient amnesia is when we forget what someone else has done for us, or a particular event, or that we owe money or a favor to someone else. We move from convenient amnesia to acting like we are in life by our might and energy, and we do not owe anyone anything. It is amazing what the human mind and heart can conceive and believe. The story below is how convenient amnesia can be displayed in our everyday lives. Maybe you have witnessed or practiced convenient amnesia at some point in your life.

J. T. was a nice guy. He loved people and learning, but had this crazy notion that no one could do anything without him. In fact, he believed that if he was not there, things would not get done. J. T. had a severe case of convenient amnesia that began when he was a child. While growing up, a friend in the neighborhood would give him money for the ice cream truck, but J. T. would not share with his younger sister and brothers. He told them that it was his ice cream and no one else could have any. Because someone else had shared with him and he seemed to be such a fun and friendly person, it surprised everyone that he responded in this way. However, J. T. forgot that, because someone had shared with him, he needed to do so with others. It is not that J. T. did not share at all, but there were times when his stinginess was pronounced.

As J. T. grew older, he thought that no one in his family had helped him achieve the high goal of magna cum laude in high school or summa cum laude in college. He thought no one else had received what he termed a "real" degree from a "real" university before he did. After all, J. T. had attended Yale and the other family college graduates graduated from historically Black colleges. In view of his accomplishments, J. T. thought more highly of himself than he ought to. Yet, he was usually able to cover up his arrogance and haughtiness with fake smiles and phony hugs.

J. T. reminded himself of how he used to be—his notorious pride—every now and then and how he was brought back to reality. It kept him humble to recall how he thought that he had pulled himself up by his own bootstraps. One day, at a Sunday dinner honoring his 85-year-old grandmother, he learned a valuable lesson. It was a lesson that has left an indelible imprint on his memory. He discovered that his family history was written in pain and unfilled dreams of those who gave up opportunities or suffered humiliation so that he and his college and business minded family members could thrive.

His grandmother told him about his great-grandfather's father, Melvin, who worked as an elevator operator for a company and knew more about the finance department than the head financial officer. In fact, the finance officer ran ideas past Grandpa Melvin and asked him questions about accounting and finance.

J. T.'s family shared story after story about those who gave so much, but received so little. Subsequently, he realized that he had not received good grades, a chance to work, a family, fun, and friends without his family or God. The bootstraps on the boots that he thought he pulled up by himself were only made available because of those who had gone on before him and around him. J. T. learned that he must be grateful and should never think that he had done everything by himself and for himself.

He smiled knowing that he never had any boots or bootstraps to pull on, but only the gifs of life, knowledge, love, family, and so much more—God.

A WORD FROM THE LORD
SCRIPTURE: Matthew 25:14–26, 28

PLACES: Capernaum, Galilee, Jerusalem, Judea

CHARACTERS: God, servants (3)

Matthew 25:14, NLT "Again, the Kingdom of Heaven can be illustrated by the story of a man going on a trip. He called together his servants and gave them money to invest for him while he was gone. **15** He gave five bags of gold to one, two bags of gold to another, and one bag of gold to the last—

dividing it in proportion to their abilities—and then left on his trip. **16** The servant who received the five bags of gold began immediately to invest the money and soon doubled it. **17** The servant with two bags of gold also went right to work and doubled the money. **18** But the servant who received the one bag of gold dug a hole in the ground and hid the master's money for safekeeping. **19** "After a long time their master returned from his trip and called them to give an account of how they had used his money. **20** The servant to whom he had entrusted the five bags of gold said, 'Sir, you gave me five bags of gold to invest, and I have doubled the amount.' **21** The master was full of praise. 'Well done, my good and faithful servant. You have been faithful in handling this small amount, so now I will give you many more responsibilities. Let's celebrate together!' **22** "Next came the servant who had received the two bags of gold, with the report, 'Sir, you gave me two bags of gold to invest, and I have doubled the amount.' **23** The master said, 'Well done, my good and faithful servant. You have been faithful in handling this small amount, so now I will give you many more responsibilities. Let's celebrate together!' **24** "Then the servant with the one bag of gold came and said, 'Sir, I know you are a hard man, harvesting crops you didn't plant and gathering crops you didn't cultivate. **25** I was afraid I would lose your money, so I hid it in the earth and here it is.' **26** "But the master replied, 'You wicked and lazy servant! You think I'm a hard man, do you, harvesting crops I didn't plant and gathering crops I didn't cultivate?

25:28 Take the money from this servant and give it to the one with the ten bags of gold.

BACKGROUND
NAME: Servants (3)
FAMILY ORIGIN: Unknown
AGE: Unknown
MARITAL STATUS: Unknown
OCCUPATION: servants
CHILDREN: Unknown
RESIDENCE: Jerusalem, or Capernaum, or Galilee, or Judea

One of the familiar ways that Jesus used to communicate was through parables. A parable is a comparison or simile. It is specifically a short narrative making a moral or religious point by comparison with natural or homely things: the New Testament parables. Our Scripture for today is parable that Christ shares about the kingdom of God. He told about H kingdom using a parable of the Talents (money, given to the slaves).

The parable of the Talents comes after the parable of the Ten Virgins. Th talent parable is one of the parables listed in the book of Matthew. Becaus of the definitive negative action of the master toward the servant who d not bring a good return on the master's money, Matthew and other gosp writers thought of this parable as "the parable of the Harsh Master." Th irresponsible servant buried what he had been given, and received th rebuke of his master (Coogan, et. al. 2001, 47). The title of the harsh mast is found in the last few verses of this parable (Matthew 25:27–30). Also co sider for a moment that the title, "harsh master," could have come from th fact that the servant told the master that he knew the master's wealth wa derived from his (the master) stealing or receiving money that he had n worked for (Matthew 25:24–25).

Matthew begins this parable of the talents with Jesus giving an accou of a very rich man, who owned slaves and had planned a trip. He called h servants together to tell them of his plans. His plans included each of the receiving a certain amount of talents (money). One received five talent one two talents, and the other one talent (Matthew 25:15). Each talent re resented "a large sum of money and was equal to the wages of a day labo er for 15 years" (Keck 1995, 453). Later in the Middle Ages, the word *tale* in English, became known as the "God-given abilities"—gifts and graces that we use in the church today (1995, 453). Also, the talent was equal "30,000 denarii (a denarius was a day's wage for a laborer)" (Coogan, et. 2001, 47).

Matthew 25:16–23 tell how each invested the money that had been giv to him. The two who had received the most both invested the money a doubled the five talents to ten and the two talents to four (vv. 16–17). T servant who received one bag dug a hole and hid his bag for safekeepir He received no investment on the money, but he did not lose or squanc the money either (v. 18). Eventually, the rich master returned and wanted know what the slaves had done with the money he had given them (v. 1 All three must have had the financial aptitude and skill to handle financ transactions (Coogan, et. al. 2001, 47), but only two acted upon them.

The servants proudly shared what they did with the money and t investments they received. Based on his response to the rich master, seems odd now that the third man would think his choice was a good one. With his response, in verses 24 and 25 and with how he hid the money, he actually believed he was making the best decision.

In church, we very seldom discuss the implications of why the servant responded as he did or how the master could be justified in his response, especially when we compare how one servant, in Matthew 18:23–35 and 24:45–51, is "forgiven for owing a lot of money and then condemns someone who owes him money."

In Matthew 25:26, the master lashed out at the servant with the one talent for not being responsible with his money. Because he did not do something to produce a greater reward and return on the master's investment, the master even called him "lazy." Additionally, in the parables, Matthew emphasized the theme of the kingdom of heaven and living the life that reflects the kingdom. This parable ends in verse 30 (NLT) with the master saying, "Now throw this useless servant into outer darkness, where there will be weeping and gnashing of teeth."

Note that the stories or parables written in the gospel of Matthew do not always have positive endings (Keck 1995, 452). Matthew's endings share how the result of not being prepared for the kingdom of heaven leaves us left out of experiencing the joy of heaven.

The following questions beg to be asked: "What are we investing in and what return are we expecting? Has God's investment in us been wasted or are we maximizing our return as much as possible?"

SOMETHING TO THINK ABOUT . . .

A readiness to do what needs to be done is paramount in life. This Bible story very much speaks to our individual preparation and how excuses are *not* always acceptable, or accepted, even if they are legitimate. What are some areas in our lives, individually and collectively, that we need to better prepare and also eradicate the negative? For example, many of us prefer to stay in relationships that are dysfunctional and keep us from moving forward.

If Jesus came today and asked if we were ready to be healed of whatever keeps us bound, how would we answer with our words and with our actions? Matthew writes throughout the gospel in various ways, "Talk is cheap if our actions do nothing to back it up." The slave in the story was given an opportunity to make an investment, but he chose not to. What are the areas that we need to invest in that we dig a hole for or cover up?

The servant in the parable decided that since he was not always a businessman of integrity, the rich man did not deserve to receive any more money. The servant surmised that the master did not need any more or deserve any more than what he had. His insolent behavior and the disrespectful way that he approached the rich man caused him grave consequences.

This servant's actions remind us that people in positions of power and who have money expect others to care for their money with great enthusiasm. In my seminary, a professor once shared that the educational system in this country is designed to protect the wealthy and grow their companies.

One of the great African American classic books is The Mis-education of the Negro, written by Carter G. Woodson in 1933. It has this famous line: "When you control a man's thinking, you do not have to worry about his actions. You do not have to tell him not to stand here or go yonder; he will find his 'proper place' and he will stay in it. You do not need to send him to the back door. He will go without being told. In fact, if there is no back door, he will cut one for his special benefit." This observation still rings true today. When we look at the biblical story and how we also make choices that result in not using our gifts or the opportunities that could lead to the freedom that we hoped for, Woodson's words are loudly proclaimed.

In the story, the servant allowed the assessment of his master to govern his actions. Even though he may have been right about how the rich man made his money, it was not the right time to share his belief. We find that we often choose to be controlled by thoughts and ideologies that feed some strange notions into our spirit that we believe we must immediately act upon. Choosing to follow these thoughts allows us to create our "back" doors and a separate "front" door entrance that make us feel comfortable.

Our investment in those things that encourage us to reach wider and higher becomes diminished. Instead, we build on those things that give us satisfaction for the moment. These are not always the best choices.

It is not wrong to have material goods, but we must caution ourselves against accumulating so much that our debt ratio keeps us living as sharecroppers. Many of us are always buying goods and services at a high interest rate that we cannot pay off the debt in a short amount of time. Therefore, we owe the lender regularly. Because we cannot timely pay off the debt due to the high interest rates, we become a slave to the lender. Thus, unless we come up with a plan to stop spending so much and stick to it, we will continue in our economic slavery. What's in your wallet—extra cash or extra unnecessary credit cards?

In addition, what is our education return? When thinking of the investment we put into education, many of us proclaim its importance. Others share with pride that they are the first or one of the few African Americans who graduated from a certain school, or in the family, or achieved in a particular field. The question begs to be asked, "When will we stop being the first or one of the few African Americans who have accomplished or achieved in a field, and have a plethora of those who have accomplished— so much so, that we can hardly count the number?" However, we must now face the reality that our public school system's failure rates for males and females are astronomical.

When our children drop out or fail in school, we are faced with many problems and issues that eat away at the core of our lives. Learning to read, write, and do math are still basic principles that we must master and pass on to the next generation. It is true that we live in a visual and technological society (i.e., cell phones, iPods, DVDs, video games, PlayStations, CDs, TVs, computers). These will one day be obsolete and considered dinosaurs by future generations. Yet the need to read, write, and do math is very crucial to creating, selling, and using these materials. On the surface, it appears that we do not need the basic learning tools, but this is not completely true when we look behind the glitz and glamour of having them. Someone receives a paycheck and money exchanges hands between people who plan, build, and sell these items. Reading, math, writing, and science are included in all of these products. The websites to describe and buy these products are created and signed off by people who have some, if not all, of the basic skills listed above.

The need to encourage and assist more African American students to graduate and provide more educational support to children and youth should remind our churches and professionals that we cannot assume that everyone can read and write, so announcements and programs need to be shared verbally or in very creative ways to reach everyone. Why is it that we cannot use the skills of music and sports to promote more reading, math, writing, and science among our people? It is amazing how many African American children who can read, write, and speak English well are considered "acting White." It is still amazing that we keep carving out the back door of "feeling less than" for someone else to walk through and perpetuate the belief that anything or anyone that is smart is White.

Slaveholders made and also passed laws to ensure that it was illegal f
slaves to learn how to read and write. Virginia was the first slaveholdi
state to pass such a law. Other states rallied around this as well. The slav
holders feared that the slaves would learn more and feel even more empo
ered to fight for their freedom. However, the church was one of the foun
ing bedrocks for education in this country. After slavery, many church
began education programs for the ex-slaves.

We have to continuously fight against the image and belief that we a
not as smart or equal to other people. This perception continues today. T
national high school graduation rate for "White students was 78%, co
pared to 72% for Asian students, 55% for African American students, a
53% for Hispanic students" (Greene and Winters 2006, 1). "Female studer
graduate high school at a higher rate than male students" (2006,
Between African American and Hispanic students, 59% of African Americ
females graduated compared to 48% of African American males, and 58%
Hispanic females graduated compared to 49% of Hispanic males (2006,

A high school diploma provides the opportunity for students to increa
their knowledge and to enter college. Persons with college degrees, in ge
eral, not only earn more than those who do not have college degrees, b
the social and health benefits are more positive as well. According
Kathleen Porter, "high school graduates earn an average of $1.2 millic
associate's degree holders earn about $1.6 million; and bachelor's degr
holders earn about $2.1 million" (2002, 1).

A DOER OF THE WORD

We need to set up more after-school programs and incorporate ma
science, and writing in our Bible study programs. For example, chapter 1
the book of Genesis—the Creation story—gives several opportunities
talk about various forms of creation. Lessons can be taught on how light
created, how the moon shines, the brightness of the sun, and how water
created. Information can be found on websites and incorporated into t
lessons.

These lessons would help children in school and maybe even spar
child's imagination to learn more and invent something related to the le
son to help others. Adults can also learn new information or revisit wh
they have already learned. Subsequently, they can share with others a
help to unlock some of the mysteries of God's creation to us.

Education is a necessary and vital part of our lives. What will we do to keep our people from wanting to create back doors and helping to knock down the locked front doors? We have made much progress as a people, but we have to keep "pressing toward the mark of the high calling of God, which is in Christ Jesus" (Philippians 3:14, paraphrased).

PRAYER

Dear Gracious God, help me to learn how to prepare and learn from others who are prepared. Grant me the tenacity and the wisdom to do what I need to do—to accept You in my life. Help me to go beyond what I see and to trust You, Jesus, to guide me. Lord, allow the Holy Spirit to dwell in my heart and my life, and lead and guide me every step of the way. Order my steps, Lord, so that I am able to walk in Your gracious Spirit and not in my own understanding. I pray all this in the peace and grace of Jesus. Amen.

BIBLIOGRAPHY

"African American Health: Current Statistics on African American Health—AIDS Section." Net Wellness Consumer Health Information Website, July2002. http://www.netwellness.org/healthtopics/aahealth/introduction.cfm (accessed February 21, 2007).

Akeelah and the Bee. Lions Gate, 2006.

Barker, Kenneth, Donald Burdick, John Stek, Walter Wessel, and Ronald Youngblood, eds. *The NIV Study Bible*. Grand Rapids, Mich.: Zondervan, 1995.

Breneman, Mervin, ed. *The New American Commentary—Ezra, Nehemiah, Esther*. Nashville, Tenn.: Broadman & Holman Publishers, 1993.

"Cancer Answers: African Americans and Cancer." Georgia Cancer Specialists Website, January 17–23, 2005. http://www.gacancer.com/canceranswer/2005/africanamericans.html (accessed February 26, 2007).

"Cancer Health Disparities: Fact Sheet." National Cancer Institute Website, November 30, 2005. http://www.cancer.gov/cancertopics/factsheet/cancerhealthdisparities (accessed February 22, 2007).

Coogan, Michael D., Marc Z. Brettler, Carol A. Newsom, Pheme Perkins, eds. *The New Oxford Annonated Bible with the Apocrypha, New Revised Standard Version*. 3rd ed. New York: Oxford University Press, 2001.

"Dr. Percy Julian (1899–1975)." Black History Pages Website. http://www.blackhistorypages.net/pages/pjulian.php (accessed February 21, 2007).

Greene, Jay P., and Marcus A. Winters. "Leaving Boys Behind: Public High School Graduation Rates." Manhattan Institute for Policy Research Website, April 2006. http://www.manhattan-institute.org/html/cr_48.htm (accessed February 21, 2007).

Haley, Alex. *Roots: The Saga of an American Family*. Reissue edition. New York: Doubleday Books, 1976.

Haney, Craig, and Philip Zimbardo. "The Past and Future of U.S. Prison Policy. Twenty-five Years After the Stanford Prison Experiment." *American Psychologist* 53 (July 1998).

Heron, Ph.D., Melonie P., and Betty L. Smith. "E-stat Deaths: Leading Causes for 2003." Center for Disease Control and Prevention Website, December 2006. http://www.cdc.gov/nchs/data/hestat/leadingdeaths03_tables.pdf#3 (accessed February 21, 2007).

Historical Society of Oak Park and River Forest Website, 2003. http://www.oprf.com/oprfhist/julianp.htm (accessed February 21, 2007).

Iammarino, Ph.D., Nicholas K. "African Americans & Cancer." Intercultural Cancer Council (ICC) Website, May 2001. http://iccnetwork.org/cancer-facts/cfsl.htm (accessed February 21, 2007).

"Incarcerated America: Human Rights Watch Backgrounder." Human Rights Watch Website, April 2003. http://www.hrw.org/backgrounder/usa/incarceration (accessed February 21, 2007).

Keck, Leander E., ed. *The New Interpreter's Bible: Matthew to Mark*. Vol. VIII. Nashville, Tenn.: Abingdon Press, 1995.

Kenyon, Kathleen Mary. *Jerusalem, Excavating 3000 Years of History*. New York: McGraw-Hill, 1967.

Life Application Study Bible, New Living Translation. Wheaton, Ill.: Tyndale House Publishers, 1996.

Major, Clarence, ed. *Juba to Jive: A Dictionary of African-American Slang*. New York: Penguin Books, 1994.

N.S., Millie. *Women of the Last Supper: We Were There Too*. InstantPublisher.com, 2003.

"People of Color and the Prison Industrial Complex: Facts and Figures at a Glance." Legal Services for Prisoners with Children Website. http://www. prisonerswithchildren.org/pubs/color.pdf (accessed February 21, 2007).

Pfeiffer, Charles F., Howard F. Vos, and John Rea, eds. *Wycliffe Bible Dictionary*. Peabody, Mass.: Hendrickson Publishers, Inc., 1988.

Plimoth Plantation, Inc.: Living Breathing History Website, June 1, 2003. http://www.plimoth.org/learn/education/kids/homeworkHelp/pilgrims.asp (accessed February 21, 2007).

Porter, Kathleen. "The Value of a College Degree." ERIC Digest, ERIC Clearinghouse on Higher Education. Washington, DC, 2002.

Roberts, Chris. *Heavy Words Lightly Thrown: The Reason Behind the Rhyme*. New York: Gotham Books, 2005.

Smith, Jessie Carney, and Joseph M. Palmisano, eds. *The African American Almanac*. Detroit: Gale Group, 2000.

Sutton, Charyn. 'Watch Night.' Mayme Clayton Library and Cultural Center Website, August 2004. http://www.wsbrec.org/blackfacts/WatchNight.htm (accessed February 22, 2007).

Woodson, Carter G. *The Mis-education of the Negro*. San Diego: Book Tree, 2006. First published in 1933.

Yaconelli, Michael. *Messy Spirituality*. Grand Rapids, Mich.: Zondervan, 2002.

NOTES